Making Drums

Dennis Waring

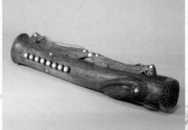

STERLING PUBLISHING CO, INC. NEW YORK

A Sterling/Tamos Book

A Sterling/Tamos Book

Published in paperback in 2006 by Sterling Publishing Co., Inc.
387 Park Avenue South, New York, NY 10016-8810
© 2003 Dennis Waring
Tamos Books Inc., 300 Wales Avenue, Winnipeg, MB, Canada R2M 2S9

Distributed in Canada by Sterling Publishing Co., Inc.
C/o Canadian Manda Group, 165 Dufferin Street
Toronto, Ontario, Canada M6K 3H6
Distributed in the United Kingdom by GMC Distribution Services,
Castle Place, 166 High Street, Lewes, East Sussex, England BN7 1XU
Distributed in Australia by Capricorn Link (Australia) Pty Ltd.
P.O. Box 704, Windsor, NSW 2756 Australia

Design by S. Whitehouse
Photography by Jerry Grajewski, Grajewski Fotograph Inc.,
Winnipeg, Canada

Printed in China

National Library of Canada Cataloging in Publication Data
Waring, Dennis, 1944-
  Making drums/Dennis Waring.

10 9 8 7 6 5 4 3 2 1

Library of Congress Cataloging-in-Publication Data
  "A Sterling/Tamos book".
  Includes index.
  ISBN 1-895569-90-7
  1. Drum--Construction. I. Title.
ML1035.W37 2003   786.9'1923   C2003-910580-6

Tamos Books Inc. acknowledges the financial support of the Government of
Canada through the Book Publishing Development Program (BPIDP) for our
publishing activities.

Special thanks to Martin Kwaku Kwaakye Obeng for access to his drum collection
as listed here: Atumpan Drum, inside front cover; Breasted Drum, p7; Akampa Drum, p11;
Nyabinghi Drum, p12; Brekete Drum, p12; Apentema Drum, p13; Sogo Drum, p18;
Sogo, Kidi and Kaganu Drums, p23; Rawhide Drum Heads, p30; Sogo, Kidi and Kaganu
and Haitian Drums, p33; Opreten Drums, p35; Brekete Drum, p36; Empty Donno Drum, p37;
Nyabinghi Drum, p77; Collection of Carved Drums, p78; Atumpan Drum, p79; Empty
Donno Shell, p81; Breasted Drum, back cover

Note: If you prefer to work in metric measurements, to convert inches to
millimeters multiply by 25.4.

The advice and directions given in this book have been carefully checked, prior to
printing, by the Author as well as the Publisher. Nevertheless, no guarantee can be given
as to the project outcome due to the possible differences in materials. Author and Publisher
will not be responsible for the results.

Sterling ISBN-13: 978-1-895569-90-2 Hardcover
    ISBN-10: 1-895569-90-7

    ISBN-13: 978-1-895569-81-0 Paperback
    ISBN-10: 1-895569-81-8

For information about custom editions, special sales, premium
and corporate purchases, please contact Sterling Special Sales
Department at 800-805-5489 or specialsales@sterlingpub.com.

Acknowledgements

A very special thank you to the following companies for supplying products used to create the projects in this book:

For leather and suede hides, as well as tooling leather, leathercrafting supplies, and tools: Tandy Leather Company®/ The Leather Factory®, Fort Worth, TX 76119, 1-800-890-1611 or 1-877-LEATHER www.tandyleather.com

For rotary cutter, cutting blades (decorative and otherwise), and clear acrylic ruler: FISKARS, 7811 W. Stewart Ave., Wausau, WI 54401, www.fiskars.com

For handles, purse frames, and canvas purses and totes: BagWorks, Inc., 3301-C South Cravens Road, Fort Worth, TX 76119, www.bagworks.com

Baglady Press, Inc., P. O. Box 2409, Evergreen, CO 80437-2409, Toll Free (US and Canada): 888-222-4523, Telephone: 303-670-2177, www.baglady.com

For fabric and gem adhesives: Beacon Adhesives Co., www.beaconcreates.com

For fabric and faux leather trims: Wrights, West Warren, MA 01092, 877-597-4448, www.wrights.com

For rubber stamps: Hampton Art, LLC, www.hamptonart.com

For beading wire and crimp beads: Beadalon®, www.beadalon.com

For acrylic paint: Plaid Enterprises Inc., www.plaidonline.com

Acknowledgements

Particular thanks are due the following people for generously allowing me to document their drum making procedures: Matthew Broad, Giovanni Ciarlo, Patrick Cooperman, Jim Dina, Paul Gemme, Nathaniel Hall, and Shari Zabriskie.

And appreciation to the following institutions and companies for their support: Everyone's Drumming Co. of Putney, Vermont; The Cooperman Co. of Bellows Falls, Vermont; Wesleyan University of Middletown, Connecticut; The New Britain Youth Museum of New Britain, Connecticut; Brattleboro Clayworks of Brattleboro, Vermont.

Gratitude also goes to Charles E. Derby for allowing me to photograph drums selected from his unique instrument collection, and Scott Kessel and Kweku Kwaakye Obeng for access to their collection of African and Caribbean drums.

Particular thanks to Susan Rosano for her computer assistance and general support. My additional thanks goes to the following people for their contributions, inspiration, and advice throughout the writing of this book: Gregory Acker, Abraham Adzenyah, Kurt Blanchard, Bob Bloom, Alvin Carter, Jonathan Deitch, Jim and Patsy Ellis, Philip Galinsky, Royal Hartigan, Chris Jones, Don Laurendeau, David Magnuson, John Marshall, Don Moore, Shaun McGinnis, Baba Olatunji, Deborah Pfeiffenberger, Kathleen Sartor, Soli Soma Drum Ensemble, Fred Stubbs, Sumarsam, and my brother, George Waring.

Photograph Credits: Dennis Waring and Susan Rosano

Preface

This book salutes some of the myriad ways, ancient and contemporary, that craftsmen have devised to construct drums. The undertaking is more complex than you may imagine since many drums are considered sacred objects, are often culturally unique, are labor intensive, and the techniques used to make them are often the "trade secret" of makers who are wary of potential competitors.

Yet, drums are probably one of the oldest musical instruments. The celebration is that drum makers through the ages have found so many meaningful, resourceful, and artful ways to manifest the simple idea of stretching a membrane on a vessel. The situation becomes more complex, however, when we consider that instruments must be made to meet the exacting standards of musicians who will use them and audiences who will hear them.

Every drum has its own idiosyncrasies. Drums can be moody. Those with natural skins react to environmental conditions, especially moisture. Room acoustics can be either supportive or suppressive to a drum's sound. Drums have personalities and players must learn how to coax the best sound from their instruments by constantly tuning and adjusting them for optimal resonance and tone. Of utmost importance to makers of all instrument types is how they sound. The allure is in the sound. The quest for the best sound has absorbed instrument makers and musicians for millenniums. Drums should sound good even in the hands of a novice.

Ultimately, it is up to makers and drummers to craft and play instruments in musically and socially meaningful ways. Drums are more than just mere musical tools, they are a means for expressing one's personal and communal place in the world. And perhaps most importantly, drumming is fun. To drum with others is extremely stimulating and powerful. And to actually construct the drum is the greatest pleasure of all.

The intent of this book, however, is not so much a step-by-step set of instructions on how to build drums but rather an overview of principles about drum making and how professional drum makers actually make drums. To this end, I solicited information from two small drum manufacturing companies, five independent drum makers including myself, a myriad of drummers, and was given access to several drum collections.

For those who wish to build a drum there is more than enough information. It helps to have a few basic woodworking tools and some woodworking experience. A table saw, jointer, and sander make drum building quite a bit easier and more efficient. But in the final analysis, with a little persistence and patience, anyone can make a drum. The facts and procedures found in the following pages will insure success.

Table of Contents

Introduction

1

Rhythm is primal. To a large extent, the rhythmic urge is fundamental for all species—animal and insect alike. Although no one knows exactly how or why nature's rhythms were organized by humankind into music, it is not unlikely that the rhythms of insects, birdsong, and other natural soundings may well have inspired this propensity. Whatever the motivation, clapping one's hands together or stamping the ground in primal dance are natural impulses for the human species. Further rhythmic organization probably resulted from communal work rhythms, and in time the relationship of rhythm and bodily movement became appealing and important. Regardless of its genesis, rhythm is universal, powerful, and an essential element of musical expression.

The drum, of course, is the most noteworthy tool for rhythm making (*fig 1*). Early people doubtless turned their exceptional tool-making ability to harnessing sound in the service of rhythm by making percussive devices. Within this large group of instruments for shaking, scraping, tapping, rubbing, and striking evolved a subgenus of instruments that featured hollow vessels covered with membranes and vellums. Although some drums (log drums, for example) have no skin covering, those with skins are the ones that we commonly recognize as real drums (classified as membranophones, where the membrane does the vibrating to initiate the sound). It is this branch of the percussion family with which this book is concerned.

Because drums are made from perishable materials (unlike prehistoric bone flutes and scrapers), we will never know the time or origin of the first drums. The earliest actual documentation that shows drums and drum playing is seen in Mesopotamian artwork (3,000 B.C). Archeologists have also found Babylonian statuettes holding and playing frame drums (2,000 B.C). Historically, drums were concerned with all aspects of cultural life and often associated with royalty as a symbol of power and prestige.

Introduction

Globally, drums make a fascinating study. I will use examples of instruments selected from many cultures to illustrate certain points or clarify particular techniques. Viewed cross culturally, the seemingly simple task of attaching a skin to a vessel is actually an extremely complex issue. Different music cultures have very different ideas of how to proceed with such matters depending on the nature of their resource and the ultimate function and use of the drum. But rather than get enmeshed in large ethnomusicological concerns, I have simply attempted to provide here a representative cross section of drums from around the world that personify the genius and resourcefulness of drum makers far and wide.

This also brings up the matter of names and spellings of drums. Seemingly similar drums can have very different names depending on a number of considerations. Linguistic perplexities such as the transcription and transliteration of languages, especially those in oral tradition, is another quagmire I wish to avoid. Although I have made every attempt to be precise, the matter of naming and categorizing some drums accurately can be tricky. Names and spellings can differ even among scholars. The author takes full responsibility for any confusions or inaccuracies in this regard.

Academic dilemmas notwithstanding, there is little doubt that drums have been and still are used worldwide for entertainment and diversion, ritual and ceremony, dance and collective bonding *(fig 2)*. Historically, no instrument is held more universally sacred than the drum. Animist cultures in particular revere the spirit inherent in natural materials used for drum making; wood, animal resource, and decorative art come together to make a musical object that has meaning and potency. It is a relationship that goes back to shamanistic times. Readers are referred to Curt Sach's seminal volume, *The History of Musical Instruments*, for a thorough discussion of these issues.

Today, drum enthusiasts still attest to a sense of entrancement and well-being verging on the supernatural after a good drumming session. Interest in drums has never been more intense. Scholars and rockers, entertainment moguls and new age philosophers, music therapists and instrument manufacturers, are all involved in one aspect or another of the past, present, and future of drums and their rhythmic potentials.

2 Babatunde Olatunji, Master Drummer

Drum Making Basics

In spite of enormous underlying complexity, both culturally and materially, all drums share a few universal basic characteristics. At the simplest level, drums have only two parts: the head and the body. In this section, drum examples selected from around the world exemplify the many ways makers have manipulated elements to achieve particular requirements of sound and design mandated by their cultures. *Note: Drum dimensions are given as height and head diameter.*

❖ Drum ❖ Morphology

Body Basics

It is interesting that parts of drums often have names that relate to human physiology (*fig 3*). Drums have heads, bodies, waists, are footed, and sometimes imbued with masculine or feminine attributes, particularly in ensemble contexts (*fig 4*).

As mentioned, drum making has complexities that make it a challenging endeavor. Because skin thickness and tension are acoustically in direct relationship to the air enclosed within the drum body, choosing and constructing a body and preparing and attaching an appropriate skin pose design problems that need careful consideration. The following chapters will help address some of these issues.

3 Breasted Drum, West Africa 33x14; 4 West African Drum Ensemble

Drums are essentially art. Painted, carved, polished, and beautified, the amount of labor expended on embellishing drums reaches far beyond the need for sound production (*figs 5-8*). The symbolic importance of a drum's shape and decoration cannot be overemphasized.

Traditionally, drum bodies were fashioned from wood and plant material (trees, bamboo, gourds, calabash, coconut shells), also stoneware and metal. And for the drumhead, animal rawhide skin has always been the material of choice. Today, drum bodies are fashioned from modern synthetics such as plastic, fiberglass, carbon fiber, and compressed epoxyed materials. Likewise, drumheads are now made from a variety of manufactured product, especially plastic-based ones which are less susceptible to moisture and heat than animal skin. This book, however, will outline mostly traditional methods of drum making using only wood, skin, and earth resources.

5 Kendang, Indonesia 36x13; 6 Puk, Korea 10x17; 7 Voodoo Drum, Haiti 25x8; 8 Long Drum, Solomon Islands 18x3

FRAME DRUMS

Circular

Square

BARREL DRUMS

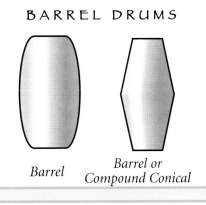

Barrel

Barrel or
Compound Conical

illustration 1
Catagories of
Drum Body Shapes

*A drum's size and shape help
determine tone quality; viewed
globally, there are numberless
variations on these basic
themes.*

GOBLET DRUMS

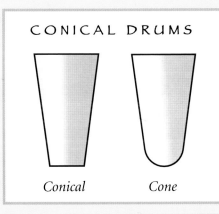

HOURGLASS/
WAISTED DRUMS

CONICAL DRUMS

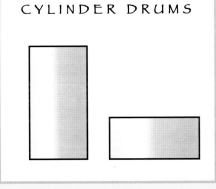

Conical

Cone

CYLINDER DRUMS

FOOTED DRUMS

KETTLE DRUMS

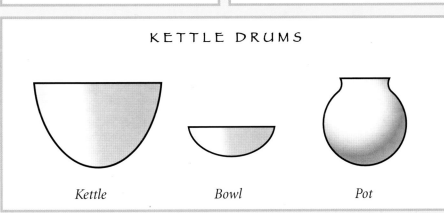

Kettle

Bowl

Pot

9

Drum Categories

Drums are usually categorized by their body shape *(illus 1 - page 9)*: frame *(figs 9-10)*, barrel *(figs 11-13)*, conical *(figs 14-15)*, goblet *(figs 16-17)*, waisted/hourglass *(figs 18-19)*, and kettle/bowl *(figs 20-22)* are common varieties. *Note: see following pages for figures.*

9 Plains Indian Drum, N. America 2x11; 10 Tamborim, Brazil 2x7; 11 Abraham Adzenyah playing Ewe Master Drum; 12 Khol, India 25x8; 13 Sogo Drums, West Africa 26x9; 14 Madala, India 14x12; 15 Congolese Drums

16 Dumbek, Middle East 14x9; 17 Goblet Drum, Middle East 12x7; 18 Ko-Tsuzumi Drums, Japan 10x8; 19 Pellet Drum, India 3x2-1/2; 20 Baya, India 11x10; 21 Nagara, Middle East, largest 10x8; 22 Akampa, West Africa 13x10

But of them all, tubular and cylindrical drums are probably the most widespread *(figs 23-29)*. These types can be further classified depending on a number of variables: interior shape, open- or closed-ended, single- or double-headed, style of base or manner of support as in footed drums *(figs 30-31)*, nature of the skin, method of skin attachment to body, and a drum's performance practice which dictates how the instrument is to be held and played (with hands or sticks or both, for example) *(figs 32-33)*.

No matter what the shape, drums come in all imaginable sizes. Comparisons of hourglass-shaped drums from places as diverse as India *(fig 34)*, Africa *(fig 35)*, and Korea *(fig 36)* reveal instruments that range in length from three inches to three or four feet. Of course, ecologies with the largest variety of trees offer drum makers the widest choice of size.

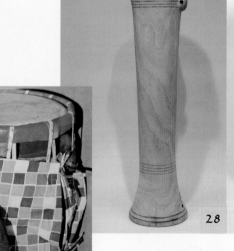

23 Pueblo Drum, North America 16x10; 24 Brekete, West Africa 14x15; 25 Tang Drum, China 6x12; 26 Daiko Drum, Japan 6x12; 27 Dhola, India 27x14; 28 Long Drum, Burma 40x8; 29 Nyabinghi, Jamaica 22x8

30

31

32

33

34

35

36

30 Footed Drum, Oceania 19x9; 31 Apentemma, West Africa 26x10; 32 Kagan, West Africa; 33 Djembe, West Africa; 34 Damaru, India 7x5; 35 Donno, West Africa 18x9; 36 Changkoo, Korea 22x18

Issues of shape and size become factors, for instance, in whether the instrument is held to or suspended from the body for mobility *(fig 37)* or supported by a stand *(fig 38)*. The stands themselves may be pieces of art as seen here with the Javanese bedug *(fig 39)*. The association of size to making high and low sounds is especially important when drums are played in ensemble *(fig 40)*.

In a general way, some drum shapes seem more characteristic to some culture worlds than others. Bowl-shaped drums *(figs 41-42)* and shallow frame drums *(fig 43)*, for instance, are more generic to Central Asia and the Islamic world.

37 Djun-djun, West Africa; 38 Cambodian Drums; 39 Bedug, Indonesia; 40 West African Drums; 41 Terbang, Indonesia 9x23; 42 Tasa Drum, Middle East 4x8; 43 Frame Drums, India, largest 3 x 17

14

Likewise, cylindrical drum shapes *(fig 44)* are more common in Europe in contrast to barrel-shaped drums which are more customary to African *(fig 45)* and Asian *(figs 46-47)* music cultures. Goblet drums are most ubiquitous in the Near and Middle East *(fig 48)* while relatively few frame drums are found in Far Eastern cultures such as China and Japan. And Latin American countries, because of the multiplicity of cultural influences, manifest a variety of drum shapes *(figs 49-52)*. Of all the variables, a drum's morphology is probably the most important element in regard to its sound.

44 Snare Drum, Europe 5x15; 45 Sogo, West Africa 26x9; 46 Kendang, Indonesia 19x8; 47 Mridangam, India 25x9; 48 Dumbeks, Middle East; 49 Tasa Drum, Trinidad 4x6; 50 Conga Drum, Latin America 31x10; 51 Bombo, South America 26x16; 52 Repinique, Brazil 11x12

53   54   55   56   57   58

Most drums, like the large goblet-shaped West African djembe *(fig 53)* and barrel-shaped Cuban conga drum *(fig 54)*, depend mostly on a large body of enclosed air for full resonance. But frame drums like the Irish bodhran *(fig 55)* and Middle Eastern bendir *(fig 56)* depend more on the body for supportive function than acoustic enhancement. Though the frame does affect the quality of sound, the thickness and tension of the skin and manner of playing are the dominant considerations here. More complex drums like the modern orchestral timpani rely on a large bowl-shaped metal body, a relatively thin skin, and fairly elaborate mechanical tuning mechanisms to function properly.

Some drums, because of a particular uniqueness, may comprise categories all their own. The adufe of Spain and Portugal and the tamalin of West Africa, for instance, are square instead of round. In other examples, the drumhead is specially modified. The rommelpot of Europe, cuica of Brazil *(fig 57)*, and khamak of India *(fig 58)* have a stick or string attached to the center of the drumhead that, when rubbed rhythmically, make a laughing/barking sound.

53 Djembes, West Africa; 54 Conga Drum, Latin America 27x10; 55 Bodhrans, Ireland 5x18; 56 Bendir, Turkey 3x18; 57 Cuica, Brazil 8x6; 58 Khamak, India 8x6

The baya of North India *(fig 59)* and other kindred drums *(fig 60)* have drumheads with multi-layered skins and a centrally-placed spot made from sticky rice paste or a paste of fine iron filings adhered to the head to affect the sound. Similarly, some long drums like the kundu drums of New Guinea require tiny balls made from spider secretions to be stuck to the drumhead for proper sounding. Trap set players likewise sometimes weight their drumheads by placing heavy tape at particular points on the membrane to modify the drum tone by diminishing excessive ring, bringing out the fundamental, or changing the blend of overtones. Twirling drums are found in a wide variety of locations, from India to the Caribbean Islands *(fig 61)*. Drums with jingles are relatively universal and comprise a family of their own *(figs 62-63)*. And Native American water drums are truly unique in the world *(fig 64)*.

59 Baya, India 11x10; 60 Madal, Nepal 15x5; 61 Twirling Drums, Various; 62 Tambourine, Europe 2x12; 63 Riq, Middle East 2x8; 64 Iroquois Drum, N. America 7x10

Drums often come in high and low pairings as with Cuban bongos *(fig 65)* and congas *(fig 66)*, East Indian tabla *(fig 67)*, and Turkish naqqara *(fig 68)*. These dual arrangements often carry symbolic significance. Some like the Latin American instruments just mentioned are, for instance, designated as masculine *(macho)* and feminine *(hembra)*. Furthermore, many African drums such as those of the West African Ewe and Ashanti music cultures are grouped into symbolic families and are often spoken of in terms of father, mother, and baby. These sets of different sized drums contribute to the overall vertical sound texture and polyrhythmic complexity of the music *(fig 69)*.

65

67

66

68

69

65 Bongo Drums, Latin America;
66 Conga Drums; 67 Tabla, India;
68 Nagara, Middle East; 69 West
African Drum Family

Nature's Resource

All competent drum makers must research and familiarize themselves with the materials necessary for fashioning a drum. Depending on the project, learning about working with wood, clay, or metal , and rawhide, becomes an obvious necessity. But of all the materials used for making drum bodies, wood is easily the material most often exploited.

However, some woods do perform better than others in certain applications. A wood's availability, ease of working, aesthetic issues, acoustical attributes, tendency to check or crack, and other deliberations come into play. Most frame drum makers in the United States, for example, prefer oak and ash for their bending qualities. And we all know that some woods are certainly easier to carve than others. Experienced instrument makers are constantly tracking down good woods and information about them.

Nonetheless, techniques and procedures often differ between makers. Bending a frame for a hoop drum, for instance, can be achieved in a number of ways: by steaming, laminating, crushing, kerfing, mitering, and bending wood green. Likewise, drum shells can be carved, stave constructed, frame-clad, or made like plywood. There are very few hard and fast rules in drum making. Therein lies the adventure.

In the final analysis, all drum makers admit that pragmatic experimentation, testing, and trial and error are the primary methods by which they refine their designs. Drum making is twenty percent science and eighty percent exploration.

One consideration that seems basic to drum morphology is the shape of the rim or bearing edge over which the head is tensioned. Since the skin must slip uniformly over the rim, it must be smooth and even all around. If the skin is not well-seated and molded to the drum body, the risk of buzzes and rattles increases. A bearing edge with surface imperfections may snag or even rip the skin as it adjusts to varying environmental conditions.

The amount of rounding and actual width of the skin-bearing portion of the rim depends on the type of drum and the desired sound. Overall, a wide bearing edge produces a fatter sound with less attack and more sustain. A thin bearing edge produces a thinner sound but with more overtones and ping. For example, frame drums like the Irish bodhran generally have a wider rim for a big resonant fundamental-heavy sound whereas a Turkish bendir adopts a thin rim for pronounced harmonics and sharper attacks.

❋A Little Science❋

Sound Basics

In the simplest of terms, long or large equals low while short or small equals high; loose equals low and tight equals high; thick equals low and thin equals high (except in the case of xylophone keys where the opposite is true). These principles are used in combination for creating a desired sound. Instrument makers must naturally master these simple fundamentals in crafting their sound-making devices.

Two more key concepts essential for making musical sound are vibration and resonance. There is no audible sensation of sound without vibration. Vibration is basically a movement of air caused by the back and forth action of an object. Sound waves are created by rarefactions and compressions between air molecules *(illus 2)*. The faster the movement, the higher the perceived frequency or pitch; slower movement makes lower sounds. Rate of vibration is expressed in cps (cycles per second) or hertz. Humans can usually hear sounds that vibrate from 20 to 20,000 cps though sounds at the ends of this spectrum are subtle and rarely heard as isolated events. Some animals hear sounds far outside this auditory envelope.

Resonance involves the enhancement of sound by forcing a contained body of air into vibration. The container itself may even contribute resonance and complexity by adding its own sympathetic vibration to the mix. Violins and guitars are good examples. A string vibrating on its own with no reinforcement will sound thin and marginally audible. Attaching it to a resonant soundbox will reinforce, amplify, and enrich the vibration. The more sympathetic the resonator is to the string, the more dynamic the sound. Much of this has to do with scientific principles of the overtone series, also called the harmonic series *(illus 3)*.

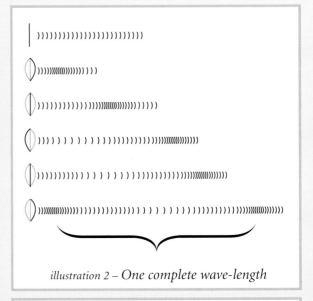

illustration 2 – One complete wave-length

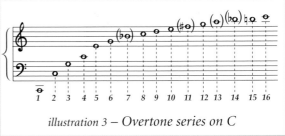

illustration 3 – Overtone series on C

In contrast to most stringed instruments, however, drum bodies are usually made from relatively inert materials that vibrate minimally. Drum sound is mostly a result of the shape and size of the drum body and the nature and tension of the drumhead.

Whatever the case, every sound we hear is essentially made up of a complex layering of vibrations all sounding at the same time. These harmonic strata are organized in measurable arrangements of overtones that are blended together by our ears into a single composite sound. The result of various blends of overtones in a sound is commonly referred to as tone quality or timbre. Generally, the more layers of vibrations, the richer the timbre *(illus 5)*.

Drum Acoustics

Although all instruments utilize vibration, resonance, and principles involving the overtone series, drums work from a somewhat different application of these natural laws than string or wind instruments. Drums actually vibrate in extremely complex ways and are capable of producing a wide spectrum of pitched and unpitched sounds depending on the relationship between the vibrating membrane, the resonating air space, and the resulting harmonic content of the sound. Drums without a clear pitch have an obscured array of overtones with much inharmonic content; drums with more decisive pitch orientation have a greater number of selectively reinforced harmonic overtones.

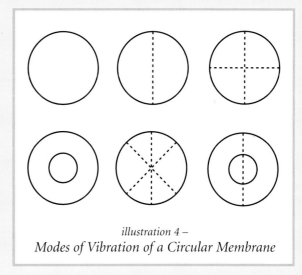

illustration 4 –
Modes of Vibration of a Circular Membrane

Drumheads vibrate in enigmatic transverse and concentric patterns that are determined by a multitude of factors. Membranes are sometimes thought of in terms of two-dimensional strings, although when coupled with a drum body, exhibit some of the additional characteristics of a vibrating column of air. Sprinkling a little fine sand on a struck membrane makes visible its vibrational tendencies— the sand will gather at areas of least vibration. The emerging patterns are called Chladni's Figures *(illus 4)*. Strings and struck membranes have areas of maximum vibration called loops and areas of minimal vibration called nodes. Whether these areas are in phase or out of phase in relationship to each other has a lot to do with a drumhead's overall mode of vibration and the resulting tonal response.

illustration 5 –
Vibration Modes of the Overtone Series in a Vibrating String

Fundamental

First Overtone

Second Overtone

Third Overtone

Combined Overtones equals Timbre

This also means that drums are not always meant to be struck directly in the center of the head as one might intuit. Hitting some drums in the middle results in a dead tone. Striking different areas of the drumhead produces very different qualities of timbre.

Drums are generally not tuned to a specific pitch, though there are notable exceptions such as the orchestral timpani and East Indian tabla. Nonetheless, drum makers always seek to maximize the relationship between the relative frequencies of the vibrating membrane to the body size and shape. Drums are most effective when the frequency of the drumhead—determined by a combination of the head's material, thickness, size, mass, and tension—is reinforced by the natural resonating frequency of the drum's interior air cavity. When a drumhead is struck, an instantaneous reaction between head and the enclosed air is initiated. The contained air is set into motion and enhanced to the extent that it can flex within its confines.

In other words, the vibrating head activates the air within the walls of the drum causing a disequilibrium of pressure inside the drum; the air is literally pumped by the vibrating head in and out of the resonating air space creating a sound characteristic to that particular style of instrument. The complexities of pressure waves within the drum decide which frequencies will prevail and determine the dominant tone of the drum. Though there is a lot more to it, all drums should possess a basic resonant fundamental sound when struck.

Drum makers and musicians sometimes attach ancillary items to their drums to further enhance the sound. Snare drums stretch a strand of wire or hide (the actual snare) across a drumhead to add a whole new dimension to its timbre, usually making the sound crisp and more pronounced. Many African drums add jingles, buzzers, and

The harmonic series is a scientifically predictable array of pitches that, in various relative combinations and strengths, determine the overall timbre or tone quality of a sound. Strings, for instance, vibrate in complex ways with multiple modes of vibration superimposed upon each other (see illustration 5). Spoken of in terms of overtones, harmonics, and partials, the overtone series gives us a description of the mathematical ratios of related frequencies and the intervalic musical relationship of pitches that encompass the complexity of a sound (see illustration 3).

rattling elements to create additional layers of sonic interest. Tambourines use jingling metal disks. Sometimes, pellets or pebbles are enclosed within the drum for added enrichment.

Naturally, the implement used to strike the drum makes a huge difference in the sound. A drum struck with hands is quite different than one struck with sticks. Drummers collect a wide array of soft to hard mallets to create many different sound qualities on certain types of drums. Hand drummers learn how and where to strike the head for maximum impact and use various hand shapes and striking techniques for variety. In general, sounds made toward the center of a drumhead are usually deeper than those produced close to the periphery or rim of the head which tend to be sharper.

Ultimately, most drums are designed through experimentation and by searching out a balance of acoustic elements that results in the most appealing sound. I refer those who wish to pursue such details to Bart Hopkin's informative book, *Musical Instrument Design: Practical Information For Instrument Design* and to other books that deal with the technical side of the nature of sound.

❖ Rawhide Drumheads ❖

Skin Basics

Hides and skins used in drum making come from a variety of animals *(fig 70)*. The most commonly used hides are from goats, deer, and calves and cows. In the past, Native Americans preferred deer, elk, buffalo, and caribou; Eskimos used the bladders of seals and walruses; snake, lizard, and other reptilian skins are common in parts of Asia; skins from large fish like sharks are used by some island cultures; traditionally, Africa has a huge choice of hides such as zebra *(fig 71)*, monkey, lion, members of the antelope family, and elephant (with some such as elephant now protected by law); and ox, pig, sheep, dog, wolf, cat, rabbit, horse, mule, donkey, rodents, animal birth sacks, and even human skin have been utilized for drumming purposes. However, the most common all-purpose skin seems to be goat because of its widespread availability, toughness, and generic thickness *(fig 72)*.

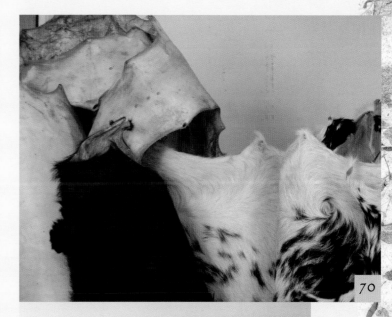

70

71

72

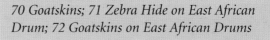

70 Goatskins; 71 Zebra Hide on East African Drum; 72 Goatskins on East African Drums

Generally, the larger the animal the thicker the skin. Larger drums usually use thick skins, small drums use thinner varieties; high-pitched drums ordinarily use thinner skins than low-pitched drums. There are, however, many exceptions to these rules. The conga drum, for instance, has a relatively small diameter drumhead opening but uses a thick cowhide with a high degree of tension to produce its characteristic tight compact sound. With the East Indian tabla and mridangam, drumheads actually use two to three layers of hide (fig 73).

Rawhide is a skin removed from an animal and left unprocessed or minimally processed. Most all drums use rawhide, not tanned hide. The Native American water drum with its tanned leather drumhead is a rare exception (fig 74). Tanned hides are processed either by hand or with chemicals to break down the skin's fibers so that the skin becomes soft and more useful as clothing, for instance.

A variety of animal rawhides are available through specialty manufacturers and retail outlets. A local slaughterhouse may also be a resource for actual unprocessed rawhide. Rawhides are also available in clarified form with the hair and fleshy tissue removed, chemically treated, excess skin trimmed and cut to specification. Some drumhead manufacturers even shave or plane hides to a uniform thickness and premount them onto a flesh hoop.

The properties that make rawhide most useful for drums is that when wet, they become flaccid, expand slightly, and conform to round shapes. There is also natural glue in wet raw skins that can be useful for securing it to a frame or vessel. When damp rawhide is attached to a drum body and allowed to dry, it more or less takes on the drum body shape and shrinks enough to tighten the skin for producing a good sound. Carefully warming rawhide will continue to tension the skin. Many folk tales tell of drummers who ritually warmed the head of their drum by the fire before it was ready to play. On the other hand, dampening a too-tight drumhead is a common way to loosen it.

73 Multi-layered Skins on East Indian Mridangam; 74 Native American Water Drum with Tanned Hide Drumhead

Animal skins also have inside and outside surfaces, a grain, and dimensionality, factors that may or may not be important for the drum maker. The hair-bearing surface usually becomes the outside of the drumhead because it has a harder finish than the inside and is more impervious to soiling. Sometimes the hair is removed from the skin by shaving it with a razor instead of scraping it. This may leave stubble that might irritate hands in some drumming styles. Also, because animal hides are usually harvested from the back of an animal, the hide often exhibits a thickened area down the backbone. The extra density creates a different shrinkage factor across the surface of the skin—the backbone pulls harder than other portions of the drumhead—thus possibly affecting the drum's tone.

Actually, rather than preparing their own drumheads, most drum makers purchase them preprocessed from companies that specialize in animal hides or through commercial leather goods dealers or mail order services.

Animal Skinning

Unless one is familiar with actual animal skinning techniques, it is probably easiest to befriend a hunter or visit a local slaughterhouse or taxidermist to find a rawhide. Removing the skin from an animal requires some skill but, when done neatly, can save a lot of effort when the time comes to use it for a drumhead.

Hide Preservation

Unless a rawhide is mounted on a drum frame soon after removal, it should be preserved before it turns green and begins to rot. Wet or damp hides should never be just rolled up for storage because they will putrefy and attract vermin. Three ways to save hides are to freeze, salt, or stretch/dry them.

Freezing is perhaps the easiest way to preserve hides. Though it is probably best to remove the hair first, hair may remain either attached or removed for long-term preservation.

Generous amounts of salt spread evenly over the hide before it is folded or rolled up will absorb the moisture in the hide and conserve it for a fairly long time. When ready to use, it is rinsed in clean water and prepared for mounting onto a drum body.

Otherwise, after removing all hair, meat scraps, fat, and fleshy tissues, rawhides are commonly stretched on a frame (*fig 75*) or nailed to a board, allowed to dry, and stored until needed.

75 Scraping Stretched Deer Hide

75

Hair Removal

Hides with very fine or close-cropped hair may not even need scraping; dense, thicker hair, however, will dampen the drumhead's ability to vibrate. Basically, hair is removed by allowing the hide to decay to the extent that hair can be easily scraped or pulled directly from the hide (*fig 76*).

For those who wish to process their own hides: Fill a large container such as a garbage can about two-thirds full with cool, not hot, water. Mix in a couple of handfuls of hydrated garden-variety lime. Immerse the skin in the brew and stir thoroughly. A lid on the container helps to contain odors. Though plain water is an effective soak, the addition of lime slows down the formation of bacteria which do the actual work of deteriorating the hair follicles. (In a practice called bucking, native peoples reached the same end by burying the skin in a dormant fire pit where the lye created by white hardwood ash loosened the hair for further processing.)

Stir the mixture every day for three or four days, maybe longer. The hide should be checked each day—by how it smells and whether a clump of hair is easily pulled from the hide by hand—to make sure it does not decompose too much. Once the skin is ready for scraping, it is spread on a firm surface and hair removal begun.

The scraping tool should not be honed sharp lest it slice or puncture the skin. A tool like a sturdy putty knife with rounded corners works well. A few trial strokes usually dictates how hard to press and whether to scrape with or against the grain. Rawhide is amazingly strong and will probably not tear or rip no matter how much pressure is applied but a firm even stroke without too much gouging is recommended.

Once the hair is removed, the hide is turned over and the remaining tissue and flesh fragments scraped from the inside, a process called fleshing. Tissue and fat can be difficult to remove and may require careful paring with a sharp knife or scissors. After dehairing and fleshing, raw skins can be immediately cut to specification and mounted on a drum body or preserved for future use as described above (*p25*) (*fig 77*).

For mounting, if the skin has been dried, it is resoaked in cool water—one or two hours for thinner skins and overnight for thicker hides—trimmed to size, and prepared for lacing. Note that the outer side of the skin has a smoother harder finish and is usually used as the playing surface. Check for any irregularities and flaws in the skin and avoid using those areas if possible.

76 Beginning Hair Removal Process; 77 Preserving Stretched Animal Hide

☙ Attaching Drumheads ☙

Securing the drumhead to the drum body is one of the most critical concerns in the construction process. There are many standard ways to do this but countless variations, even within specific cultures. The most common procedures utilize banding, gluing, tacking, pegging, lacing, or specialty hardware for tensioning *(illus 6)*.

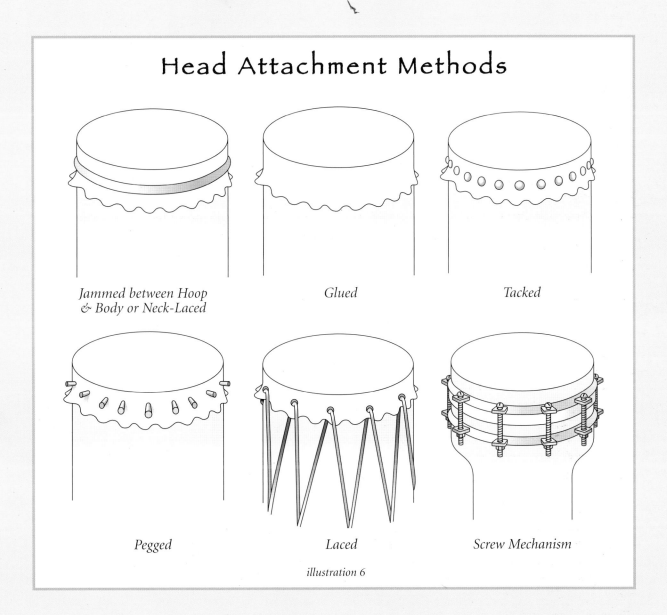

Head Attachment Methods

Jammed between Hoop & Body or Neck-Laced

Glued

Tacked

Pegged

Laced

Screw Mechanism

illustration 6

Neck-Laced Drumheads

Perhaps the easiest way to mount a drumhead is to jam the skin firmly between a tight-fitting hoop and the body of the vessel *(figs 78-79)*. This method is usually temporary and requires frequent restretching and adjustment. Alternatively, skins may be secured by wrapping a cord tightly around the neck of the vessel (fig 80). Unless the head is glued, this method also needs routine adjustment.

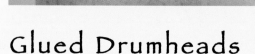

78

79

80

81

82

Glued Drumheads

Moistened animal rawhides—including mammals, fish, and reptiles *(figs 81-82)*—make their own natural glue and bond fairly well with wood or earthenware *(figs 83-84)*. In fact, hide glue, made from the hides and hooves of horses, cows, and such, has been used by violin makers and furniture makers for generations. Today, modern water-based glues are used by many drum makers.

84

83

78-79 Hides jammed between hoop and drum body; 80 Drumhead tied to drum body; 82-85 Glued drumheads

85

86

Thin skins conform and stick to round shapes fairly easily *(fig 85)* but thicker skins such as cowhide do not conform as well and remain bulky and somewhat inelastic even after soaking. With drums that are designed to be played hard, the natural gluing quality of a skin is usually strengthened with some sort of banding *(fig 86)*, lacing *(fig 87)*, sewing *(fig 88)*, pegging *(fig 89)* or tacking *(fig 90)* that attaches the skin more firmly to the drum body.

87

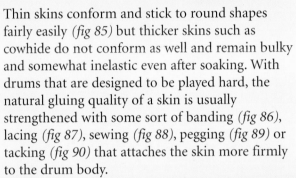

88

90

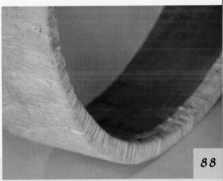

89

86 Banding; 87 Lacing; 88 Sewing; 89 Pegging; 90 Tacking

29

Tacks, Staples, and Pegs

If the drum shell is thick enough, attaching a skin using staples, nails, or sturdy tacks can be used *(figs 91-92)*. Stapling with a construction-grade staple gun is a quick easy way of securing thinner hides; staples are usually covered with a ribbon of ornamental material glued around the shell. An elaborate example of the tacking approach is used with Daiko drums of Japan as well as many other drums found throughout East Asia *(figs 93-96)*.

Small wood pegs called buttons are driven into a drum shell to secure lighter weight skins on smaller drums *(figs 97-98)*. Larger pegs are employed for drumheads that are more stressed or require adjustment *(figs 99-101)*. As with glued hides, the unfavorable aspect of stapling, tacking, or permanently pegging drumheads is that they are usually nonadjustable.

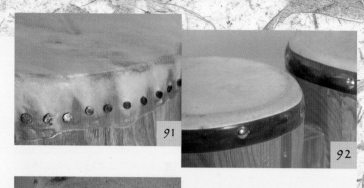

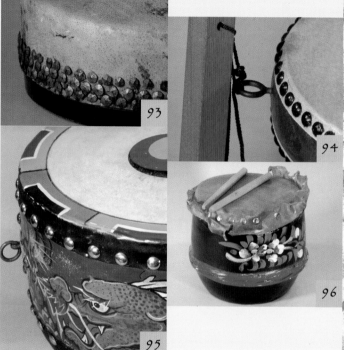

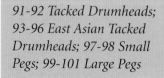

91-92 Tacked Drumheads; 93-96 East Asian Tacked Drumheads; 97-98 Small Pegs; 99-101 Large Pegs

Lacing Logistics

Lacing the drumhead to a drum body is probably the most universal attachment method. There are scores of ways to lace a drumhead. And although many traditional lacing schemes are certainly tried and true and well suited for their situations, new options and variations for attaching skins are still being developed today. The three major considerations in this process are 1) what material to use for lacing 2) how the lacing actually connects to the head and 3) how to anchor the lacing opposite the head in order to secure and tension it.

Thonging, cut strips of raw animal hide, is the most traditional and oft-used material for lacing *(figs 102-103)* though in some parts of the world rattan lacing (tough stringy vine) is more common *(figs 104-105)*. Modern materials like high-tech climbing rope *(fig 106)*, non-stretching nylon or cotton cord *(fig 107)*, and forms of twine *(fig 108)*, all of which are less prone to breaking than hide lace, are now widely-used.

Direct lacing is a simple method *(illus 7a)* where thonging is laced through holes punched directly through the skin *(figs 109-111)*; there is always the risk of the skin tearing if the hide is not thick enough or the head gets too tight. Spacing holes reasonably close together is one way to help avoid possible tearing *(figs 112-113)*.

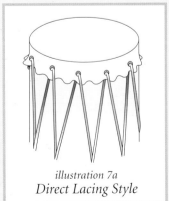

illustration 7a
Direct Lacing Style

102-103 *Rawhide Lacing;*
104-105 *Rattan Lacing;*
106 *Climbing Rope Lacing;*
107 *Nylon Rope Lacing;*
108 *Twine Rope Lacing;*
109-111 *Direct Lacing;*
112-113 *Closed Direct Lacing*

Lacing directly through skin can also be strengthened using a variety of strategies such as feeding lace through two holes instead of one *(illus 7b) (fig 114)* or weaving an extra reinforcing strand of hide through the holes to distribute the pressure and give the tensioning lace something substantial to pull on rather than the skin alone *(illus 7c) (figs 115-117)*. As well, a strand of hide, rope, vine, etc., is often stitched or woven into the skin for extra reinforcement *(figs 118-120)*.

A common way of increasing the tensioning value of thin lacing is by twitching adjacent laces as shown in the accompanying diagram *(illus 8)* and in the photographs of two Asian drums *(figs 121-122)*.

illustration 7b
Two-Hole Lacing Style

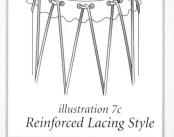

illustration 7c
Reinforced Lacing Style

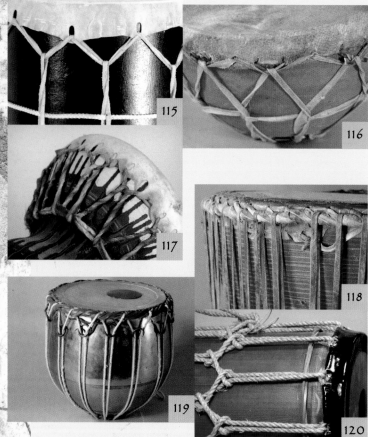

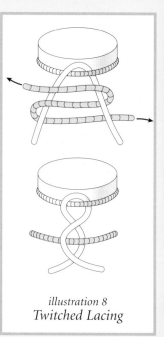

illustration 8
Twitched Lacing

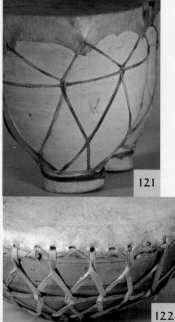

114 Two-Hole Direct Lacing; 115-117 Direct Lacing with Rawhide Lace Reinforcement; 118-120 Direct Lacing with Hoop Reinforcement; 121-122 Twitched Lacing

The Flesh Hoop

Indirect lacing is a safer method than direct lacing although more work. It involves lapping and tucking the skin around a flesh hoop (*illus 9*). The lacing is still punched directly through the skin but the flesh hoop takes the brunt of the tension rather than the skin itself.

In some ways this method is similar to sewing or stitching the drumhead onto a hoop of rawhide or rope to strengthen it. Traditionally, strands of rattan, or green branches twisted or braided into circular form have been used as drumhead frames. The difference with actual flesh hoops is that the skin is lapped and tucked onto a relatively rigid hoop material like wood or metal rather than stitched onto a hoop made of rope, sinew, or vine.

Flesh hoops are necessarily made larger than the diameter of the drum shell. Wood hoops can be bent into a circular configuration while the wood is green or by using steam (heat and water). Alternatively, wood hoops can be made by gluing thin layers of wood veneer together around a circular mold resulting in a laminated plywood ring. Metal hoops are usually fabricated is specialty shops.

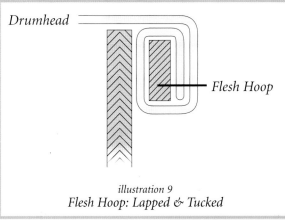

illustration 9
Flesh Hoop: Lapped & Tucked

illustration 10
Style of lacing skin mounted on a flesh hoop

Scores of the world's drums utilize the flesh hoop idea for securing the drumhead (*figs 123-126*). After the skin is lapped and secured onto the flesh hoop, the lacing is looped over the flesh hoop, punched through the skin (*illus 10*), and anchored at the opposite end.

One particularly interesting drum, the oprenten of West Africa, combines variations of the methods described above: large wood pegs, sewn-in flesh hoop, and a unique form of lacing. The body is carved from a solid piece of wood, pegs fashioned from tree branches, peg holes drilled, and the drumhead cut to size (fig 127). Cord lacing is sewn into the skin (fig 128) then cross-twisted and attached to each peg (fig 129). Hammering the pegs farther into the drum shell tightens the drumhead.

123-126 Lacing Through a Flesh Hoop;
127-129 Laced and Pegged African Drum

The Counter Hoop

Often, the flesh hoop is reinforced by an additional matching counter hoop (sometimes called a hat) of the same diameter. Most drums today use some variation of this flesh hoop/counter hoop arrangement. In the examples shown, the lacing (or tensioning hardware) is attached onto the counter hoop which in turn presses against the flesh hoop *(figs 130-133)*. This avoids having to perforate or damage the skin and the need to lap and tuck the skin onto the flesh hoop. Instead, the skin is wrapped around the flesh hoop and passed beneath the counter hoop which, as it is tensioned, binds the skin firmly in place *(illus 11)*. For hand drums such as congas, ashikos, djembes, etc., counter hoops are usually set well below the plane of the drumhead so as not to be in the way *(fig 134)*. Conversely, stick drummers usually want counter hoops slightly above the plane of the playing surface to facilitate rim shots and other effects *(fig 135)*.

130

131

132

133

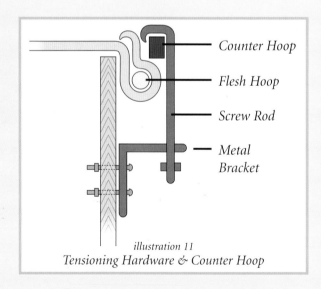

Counter Hoop

Flesh Hoop

Screw Rod

Metal Bracket

illustration 11
Tensioning Hardware & Counter Hoop

130-133 Drums with Counter Hoops; 134 Counter Hoop Set Low on Body; 135 Counter Hoop Set High on Body

Today, most drum makers use metal hoops. They are by far the strongest and longest lasting. Because making them is difficult without the proper equipment, most drum makers have their hoops manufactured to specification. The choice of round, flat, or square hoop stock is determined by the size and nature of the drum. Metal flesh hoops are usually galvanized or wrapped in cloth to prevent rust from staining the skin.

134

135

Lacing Patterns

There are a number of different variations for arranging lacing *(illus 12)*. For single-headed drums, the lacing has to attach to some sort of anchoring situation opposite the playing head. With double-headed drums, the lacing simply zig-zags back and forth between the two heads. Most common are "N" *(figs 136-137)* and "W" patterns *(figs 138-139)*.

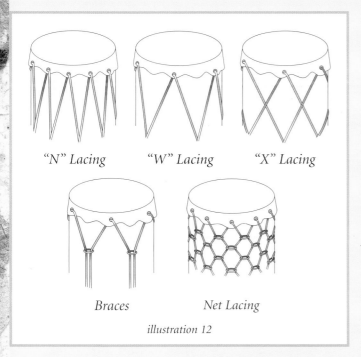

"N" Lacing   "W" Lacing   "X" Lacing

Braces   Net Lacing

illustration 12

Variations on the N and W lacing patterns include the "Y" pattern, which is like the N pattern but with sliding braces *(figs 140-141)*, and the "X" pattern. Various forms of lateral lacing also aid in tensioning *(figs 142-143)*. A drum with numerous lateral lacings is said to be net laced. There are many other idiosyncratic styles as well *(figs 144-145)*.

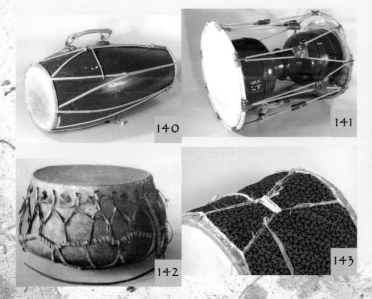

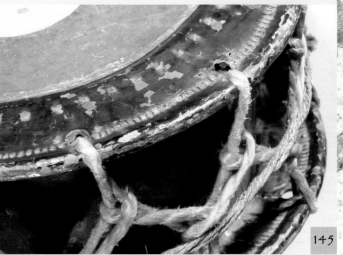

136-137 N Lacing Patterns; 138-139 W Lacing Patterns; 140-141 Y Lacing Patterns with Sliding Braces; 142-143 Lateral Lacing; 144-145 Other Lacing Styles

One interesting style of drumhead attachment is with the West African talking drum called donno (fig 146). The heads are first mounted on hoops fashioned from rattan.
Loops for the lacing are sewn directly through the hoops (figs 147-148). Since the lacing is squeezed to produce its characteristic high and low tones, a tightly configured N pattern is used to connect the two heads to the drum's body (figs 149-150).

With single-headed drums, the lacing must naturally anchor to something other than another skin or hoop. For frame drums, the lacing sometimes simply crosses over the back (or bottom) and laces to the skin on the opposite side *(figs 151-152)*. On bowl-shaped bodies, lacing may attach to a circlet of hide or a metal ring at the back of the vessel *(figs 153-154)*. Lacing for goblet and conical-shaped drums relies on a leather or metal ring mounted on the drum body opposite the head for anchoring the lace *(figs 155-156)*. The ring pulls up securely against the sloping shape of the shell as the lace is tensioned.

146-150 Lacing a West African Talking Drum; 151-152 Frame Drum Lacing; 153-154 Bowl Drum Lacing; 155-156 Goblet and Conical Drum Lacing

Adjustable Hardware

Most modern drums use some sort of metal tensioning hardware *(figs 157-159)*. Usually, threaded screw rods connect the counter hoop to some sort of bracket anchored to the drum shell *(see illus 11)*. The head is pulled tighter as the screw rod is tightened, usually with a small wrench. These mechanisms are specially designed for both single or double-headed drums. As examples, Cuban conga drums *(fig 160)*, Brazilian samba drums *(figs 161-162)*, marching band and orchestral drums *(fig 163)*, and drums used in modern day drum sets *(fig 164)*, all use fairly specialized hardware for tensioning devices. Available through percussion supply houses, they may be costly but provide the greatest flexibility for tone and tuning. There are many more unconventional varieties of hardware tensioning schemes as well *(figs 165-166)*.

157

158

159

160

163

161

162

164

165

166

157-159 Drumhead Mounting Hardware; 160 Conga Drum; 161-162 Samba Drums; 163 European Drum; 164 Modern Tensioning Hardware; 165-166 Other Tensioning Hardware

37

Drumhead Tuning

Percussionists often have to adjust and tweak the tension of their drumheads to generate the most resonant and desirable sound. Trap set drummers, for instance, tune each of their drums in relationship to each other. African drum ensembles tune drums so that complex polyrhythms produce melodies of a sort. Another example, the tabla of North India, requires extremely fine tuning to exactly match the drone pitch characteristic to that culture's music. As a rule, it is naturally advantageous to have some level of drumhead adjustability, especially if a performance is exposed to elements of weather, particularly humidity or rain, which can render a drum useless.

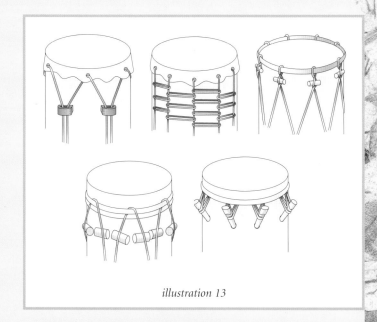

illustration 13

There are, however, many lacing designs that allow for tuning instruments without having to resort to metal hardware *(illus 13)*. When using the N or W lacing pattern, braces (sometimes called pulls, tugs, buffs, and ears) made of loops of leather, cord, or metal rings can be attached around two adjacent laces thus creating the Y pattern. Sliding the braces up pulls the laces closer together which in turn tightens the drumhead *(figs 167-169)*.

Similar in concept to braces is the net lacing style, which is simply pulling separate strands of lace together with multiple, laterally-attached leather or string loops at intervals around the drum *(see fig 143)*. The more the laces are stretched and displaced from their normal position, the more the drumhead is tensioned *(see illus 12)*.

In addition to the twitching technique shown earlier *(see illus 8 and figs 121-122)*, a similar approach uses a method whereby pairs of lacing are twitched together by inserting short sticks or dowels between adjacent strands of lacing *(as shown in the upper righthand drawing in illustration 13)*. Twisting the dowels further brings the drumhead to the desired tension.

167

168

169

167-169 Tuning with Braces

Drums such as the East Indian tabla and pakhawaj use shims or chocs. When inserted under the lacing and slid one way or the other, they act as wedges and tension the drumhead *(figs 170-171)*. In another example, the wedge principle is applied differently to hold the drumhead tightly on the body *(fig 172)*.

And as with the West African oprenten *(see figs 127-129)* and other African and Caribbean drums *(see figs 99-101)*, pegs are sometimes hammered into the drum shell in such a way as to pull the drumhead tighter.

Ultimately, the seemingly simple task of mounting a drumhead is actually fairly involved. But what is interesting are the myriad of ingenious ways drum makers have devised to do so.

170

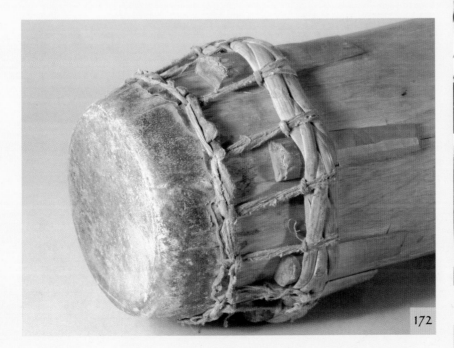

172

171

170-171 *Tuning with Chocs;*
172 *Tuning with Wedges*

✤Mali Weave✤

he so-called Mali weave has become a common method for attaching drumheads on djembes, ashikos, and other drums that require a fairly stout method of lacing. This lacing method is used in several of the building projects in this book and is included here for easy reference.

For single-headed drums, the Mali weave requires two hoops and a ring: the flesh hoop and reinforcing counter hoop for mounting the drumhead skin, and another ring mounted lower on the drum shell for anchoring the lacing. Though hoops can be made from a variety of materials, makers of high tension drums usually prefer hoops made from rolled steel welded at the joint. The flesh hoop and counter hoop are fabricated at least ½ inch larger than the outside diameter of the shell to leave room for the hide, knots, and cloth wrapping.

Knot-Tying Process

Two-inch-wide lengths of fabric, colorful or plain, are wrapped around both hoops and the anchoring ring as both a protective (against rust) and decorative element. One end of the fabric is secured to each hoop with a little tape (*fig 173*) and, while stretching it tightly, wrapped in a spiraling pattern all around (*fig 174*). The end is affixed with a little tape or glue (*fig 175*).

Preparations are then made for tying knots onto the counter hoop and the lower anchoring ring. For maximum strength, the following example of stringing an ashiko drum uses 3-mil, static-weave, rock-climbing nylon rope. The number of knots necessary is variable depending on the diameter of the drumhead and the degree of tension required to keep the head tight—more knots for a larger,

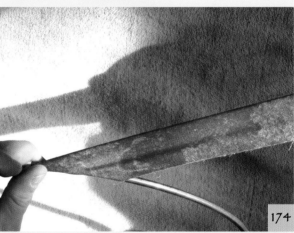

173-175 Wrapping Hoops with Cloth

tighter drumhead.

This project uses 12 knots tied equidistant around the counter hoop and anchoring ring. A round template divided into pie-shaped sections helps lay out the spacing accurately *(fig 176)*. Knotting points are marked onto the hoop with chalk, as shown *(fig 177)*.

At least 6 inches of rope are calculated per knot. In this case, the amount of rope needed to make 12 knots for a 9 inch diameter drum shell is approximately 7 feet of rope.

This first knot is tied as shown by passing the rope over the ring, back up through, under the ring, down through, and pulled tight *(figs 178-182)*. Twelve knots are then tied all around the ring *(figs 183-186)*. At the end, a square knot secures the arrangement *(figs 187-191)*. All the knotted loops are flipped to the outside of the hoop ready to receive the lacing *(fig 192)*.

The bottom anchoring ring is prepared in the same fashion with the same number of knots as the counter hoop.

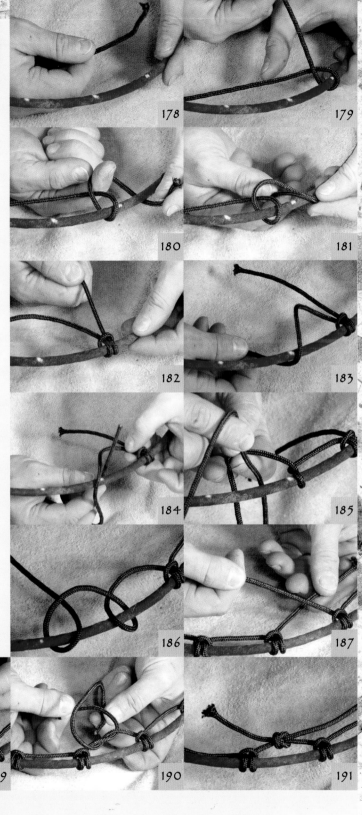

176-177 Spacing for Knots; 178-192 Knot Tying Procedure

Lapping Skin onto Hoops

The skin for the drumhead is now soaked in water until flaccid *(see Rawhide Drumheads, p23)*. The side of the skin facing out is determined and placed face down on a clean surface. The flesh hoop is placed on the skin and the counter hoop on top of the flesh hoop *(figs 193-194)*. The skin is pulled in between the two hoops *(figs 195-196)* and all wrinkles smoothed out. The assembly is now ready to position on top of the drum shell *(fig 197)*.

If the skin is unwieldy and hard to lap between the flesh and counter hoops, clothespins or even temporarily sewing the skin onto the flesh hoop helps keep it under control. For details on this procedure, see the drumhead mounting section of the Latin Drum project *(p63)*.

193

194

195

196

197

193-197 Lapping Skin Procedure

Lacing the Drumhead

The amount of rope needed to lace the instrument is determined by measuring the distance between the head of the drum to the lower anchoring ring, in this case 12 inches. The lacing passes between anchoring ring and counter hoop two times for each knot. Thus 12 knots times 24 inches equals approximately 55 feet of lacing. If using nylon cord, burn the tip of the cord to keep it from unraveling.

The rope is first laced through one of the loops on the lower ring and up through the corresponding loop on the upper ring. The rope end is then passed over and through the loop right next to it and down through the corresponding loop on the lower ring. Again, across to the next loop and back to the upper ring, and so forth *(figs 198-201)*. It is important to keep the head centered on the shell and both hoops aligned with each other throughout this operation.

198

199

200

201

198-201 Lacing Procedure

A half-hitch knot tied on the end of the rope and a slip knot *(figs 202-206)* complete the lacing pattern and allow for taking up the slack all around *(fig 207)*. Several rounds of tightening are necessary before the drumhead settles in and finds its voice. Keeping the head centered through the tightening process requires careful attention and a feel for how much to tension the skin each time around. For this style of drum, the drumhead is usually laced fairly tight.

Excess skin is now trimmed *(fig 208)* and the raw edge tucked down under the counter hoop with a dull knife *(fig 209)*. The drum is set aside in a cool place until the skin has dried. After final tightening and "tuning" is completed, the drum is ready to play.

202-206 Finishing Lacing; 207 Taking Up Slack; 208 Trimming Excess Skin; 209 Tucking Raw Edge

44

Drum Project Examples

This part of the book provides examples of how some drums are actually made by outlining actual methods used by various makers who generously allowed me to document their procedures. The information will greatly assist amateur drum makers in building their own instruments.

I have attempted to provide a cultural orientation for each of the following drum projects but it should be understood that these nationalistic designations are highly generalized. Illustrating the endless variations and complexities found even within a single drum family is a nearly insurmountable task. Nonetheless, I have attempted to stay true to the spirit of the drums' cultural origins.

Frame Drums

The frame drum family is characterized by relatively shallow-bodied frames in varying diameters with a membrane stretched over one or both sides (fig 210). The drum projects here are fairly representative of frame drums around the world. There is little doubt that basic types of frame drums enhanced the activities of humankind from earliest times. Sometimes called hoop drums, most are circular in shape, but there are those with eight (fig 211), twelve, sixteen sides, even square and triangular drums. Hoop drums, because of their circular form and ritual use, hold important symbolic significance for many cultures. Throughout history, shamanistic custom and drum making were often one and the same activity (fig 212). For most cultures, drums and other musical instruments have always been a necessity as important implements for ceremonial effectiveness toward cosmic accord.

The idea of stretching a skin on a frame is a simple concept but one that all peoples have found infinite numbers of ways to modify and fashion. Frame drums are universal in range as demonstrated by the Brazilian panderio, European tambourine, Irish bodhran, East Indian chang, North African muzzar, Native American hoop drum, Egyptian tar, Ghanian tamelin, Turkish bendir, and Siberian shaman's drum, to name but a few (fig 213). Another cross-cultural tendency is to attach metal jingles, rings, or thin circular plates to the drum frame to increase its sonic potential as seen with the Middle Eastern riq (fig 214), European tambourine (fig 215), Brazilian panderio, and East Indian kanjira.

210 Middle Eastern Frame Drums; 211 Eight-Side Mitered Frame; 212 Nepalese Shaman's Drum; 213 Bodhran, Tar, and Bendir Drums; 214 Egyptian Riq; 215 Tambourine

Making Circular Frames

One of the biggest challenges in making a hoop drum is how to bend a straight board into circular form.

1 Bending green wood requires peeling a layer of new growth wood from a tree and securing it into circular form. — used in Primitive Drum project.

2 Using water and heat to steam-bend wood in order to wrap it around a circular mold. — used in Irish Drum project.

3 Gluing layers of veneers together around a mold in plywood fashion to build up shell thickness. — used in Middle East Drum project.

4 Feeding wood through a pinch roller or a mangle of three heated rollers which compresses the wood on its inner face causing it to curl into a circle.

5 Using picture frame techniques allows building up and gluing any number of mitered segments together for a drum frame. — used in the Indian Drum project.

6 Tamboring or sawing kerfs across the width of the wood at close intervals to effectively thin the wood so that it will bend and even twist to a degree. Once formed, it is stabilized by gluing a layer of veneer to the kerfed surface.

Frame drums are usually about 16 inches to 18 inches in diameter. To determine the linear measure of wood necessary to achieve a specified hoop size, a drum's diameter is divided by pi (3.14).

With many early drums, the hoop's ends were simply overlapped and lashed together with lacing (fig 216) (see Primitive Drum, p47), or secured with nails or tacks (fig 217). Another choice is a scarf joint that involves thinning and tapering the ends so that when overlapped and glued together, they form a relatively seamless connection (fig 218) (see Irish Drum, p52).

216 Lashed Drum Frame; 217 Tacked Drum Frame; 218 Scarf Joint

216

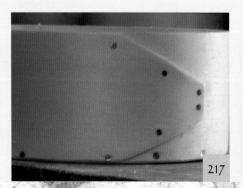

217

218

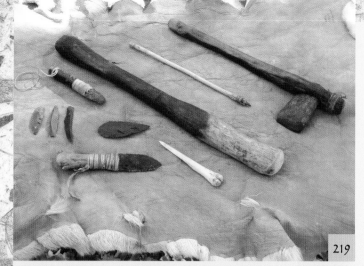

219

1 Primitive Drum

Indigenous and native cultures are often described as primitive, but I use the word simply for lack of a more recognizable term. Increasingly, we find that prehistoric societies exhibited sophistications previously unimagined. Among these ingenuities was the use of tools.

Tools have been around for an estimated two million years. Early technology comprised implements that bludgeoned, cut, sliced, and poked *(fig 219)*. But from the Upper Paleolithic Period, about 250,000 years ago, humankind witnessed a quantum leap in tool development. Highly functional tools of stone, bone, and wood were developed and used in many pursuits including making drums *(fig 220)*.

Constructing a frame drum using only stone age tools, though challenging, is not as formidable as one might think. This first hoop drum project is modeled on many early types of single-headed Native American drums and utilizes only primordial tools in its making.

220

Hide Preparation

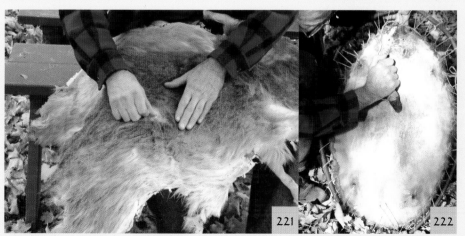

221   222

Preparing the rawhide from an animal is the first order of business *(fig 221)*. See chapter on Rawhide Drumheads for procedures. After fleshing, the skin is nailed to a board or stretched on a drying-frame where final scraping of hair and fleshy tissue is completed *(fig 222)*.

219 Stone Age Tools; 220 Drum Components & Finished Drum; 221-222 Scraping and Cleaning Hide

Drum Frame

Traditionally, ash is the usual choice of wood. It bends easily when green and its open, air-porous layer of springwood growth (called sapwood) can be separated from the tree relatively easily. Sapwood is the tree stratum of most recent growth and thus more pliable and bendable than the inner layers of older sapwood and heartwood.

First, the tree bark is removed with an ax made of a sharp stone set into a wood handle. A blaze is hewn long enough to accommodate the drum's circumference plus several inches of overlap (fig 223).

Next, a methodical beating of the exposed sapwood layer with a wooden club helps release it from its interior moorings (fig 224). Care is taken to not crush or indent the wood excessively. All the surface area intended for use receives uniform treatment.

A lateral incision is then cut or sawed into the tree at the top of the blaze. This is the beginning point of detachment (fig 225). A blade is carefully worked under the layer of sapwood as shown (fig 226). Effort is made to minimize splitting or breaking the wood although a little split here and there is hard to avoid.

223 Removing Bark with Stone Ax; 224 Clubbing Outer Layer of Tree; 225 Incising Top of Blaze; 226 Removing Sapwood Layer

227 | 228

229 | 230

Once the length of wood is removed from the tree *(fig 227)*, split or ragged ends are trimmed *(fig 228)* and holes drilled in one or both ends for lashing and securing the wood into a circular form. In this case, holes are drilled with a primitive form of drill twirled between the hands *(fig 229)*. A rawhide thong for lashing the ends together is cut with a flint razor *(fig 230)*.

The wood is then coaxed into circular shape (fig 231). If the wood resists bending fully, soaking it with hot water facilitates the process. Once the frame is formed, the ends are overlapped and lashed together with thonging as shown *(figs 232-233)*.

Making a perfect symmetrically round drum using the techniques outlined here is tricky. Since there are usually no jigs, molds, or forms involved, the final disposition of the wood and skin is at the whim of their natural tendencies. Wood and rawhide dry unevenly due to inconsistencies in grain configuration in the wood and thickness factors with the skin. Some asymmetry is normal, and has little impact on the usability and function of the drum.

231 | 232

227 Wood Blanks for Frames; 228 Trimming Ragged End; 229 Drilling Holes for Lashing; 230 Cutting Lacing; 231 Bending Drum Frame; 232-233 Lashing Drum Frame

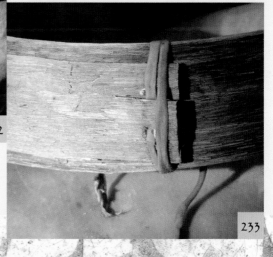

233

Drumhead Attachment

The drumhead skin is now cut to size. Skin is cut so that it fully overlaps the sides of the drum and stretches around to the back of the drum as seen with the completed drum in the accompanying photograph *(fig 234)*. Holes are poked at regular intervals with an awl, fashioned from bone *(fig 235)*. Holes poked through thinner areas in the skin are slightly farther in from the outside edge to resist tearing. This drum has 32 holes.

Additional rawhide thong for lacing is then cut for attaching the skin and making the handle. Cutting rawhide for lacing the skin to the frame can be made from wet or dry scraps of skin or cut from a fresh hide *(fig 236)*. A long continuous strand of lacing is better than too many short ones knotted together. Using a spiraling cutting pattern helps in this regard.

Both skin and lace are now soaked in cool water until flaccid (length of time depends on thickness of the skin) and kept damp throughout the process of mounting the drumhead.

The frame is placed onto the skin and string laced across the back in 12 o'clock to 6 o'clock and 9 o'clock to 3 o'clock fashion *(figs 237-238)*. From here it is a matter of continuing to connect opposite sides of the skin in a back-and-forth configuration.

234 Assaying Skin for Mounting; 235 Poking Holes with Bone Awl; 236 Cutting Lacing from Hide; 237-238 Lacing Drumhead

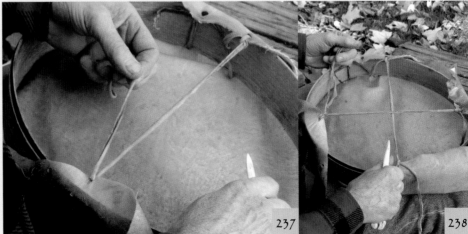

The handle is finished by pulling eight strands of lacing together into four bundles with each bundle wrapped about half their length *(figs 239-240)*. This not only helps to further tension the skin so that it will remain taut even under humid conditions but adds a great visual element to the drum *(fig 241)*. Here are two alternative handle designs *(figs 242-243)*.

Finally, drum beaters are usually made from a stick, padding, and a cloth or tanned hide covering *(fig 244)*. The drum is ready to play.

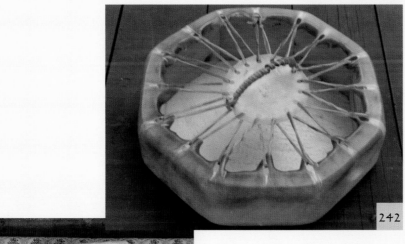

239-240 Fashioning the Handle;
241 Completed Drum Handle;
242-243 Alternative Handle Designs;
244 Drum and Beater

2 Irish Drum

The popular traditional folk drum from Ireland and the British Isles called the bodhran (bow-ran) provides a good example for examining steam-bending processes, the method by which a majority of frame drums are built today. Bodhrans are generally characterized by an 18 inch diameter circular frame, 4 to 6 inches deep, mounted with a medium to heavy goatskin head, and single or double handle set inside the drum frame *(fig 245)*. The goatskin is traditionally glued and tacked onto the frame. The bodhran is played with a tipper, a double-headed stick of variable design usually 8 inches to 10 inches long.

Milling and Steam-Bending Drum Frames

As wood is steam heated, the cellular integrity of the wood fibers is compromised to the extent that it becomes somewhat malleable under directed pressure. Wood can be bent and reshaped, however, only as long as it remains well-saturated with steam. When it cools, it quickly restabilizes. Porous woods such as ash and oak are favorites because their open cellular structures make them easier to bend and coax into new shapes.

Although drum frames can be fashioned by hand by bending dampened wood over a hot bending iron, for making perfectly round drum frames, a steam cabinet and process for wrapping wood around a circular mold are best. This basic technology has been enhanced in recent times to satisfy today's manufacturing mandates as this project shows.

First, wood is milled to specification from a freshly harvested log *(figs 246-247)*. A good sawyer proceeds methodically with an eye to which parts

245

246

247

245 Irish Bodhrans; 246-248 Milling Log Into Boards

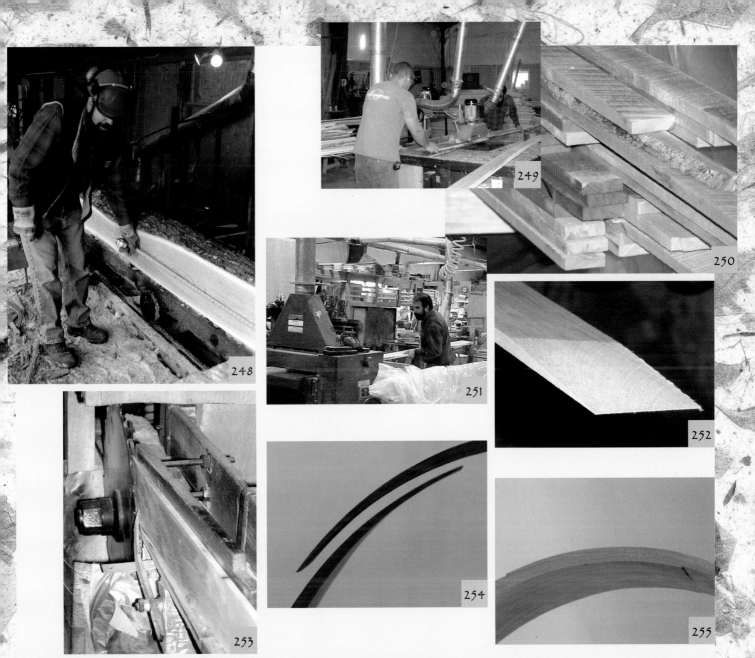

248 Sizing up a log

249 Sawing Wood to Width

250

251

252

253

254

255

of the log are best suited for particular sizes of drum frames *(fig 248)*. Wood is generally slab cut with a giant circular saw to produce boards that are straight-grained with a minimum of knots, internal checks, or aberrant grain configurations.

The lumber can be kiln-dried at this stage though it is easier to steam-bend drum frames after it is freshly milled. Bending the wood green helps to alleviate and prevent fracturing. Wood is then measured and cut into frame blanks. A table saw is used for rip-sawing stock to width *(figs 249-250)*, a radial arm saw for cross-cutting to length, and a planing machine for thicknessing *(fig 251)*.
Next, a scarf joint is formed by tapering both ends of the frame blank (fig 252). This is done either with a good miter saw, special sanding setup, or, in this case, a tapering jig on a table saw *(fig 253)*. Once joined, scarf joints allow for a fairly seamless junction *(figs 254-255)*.

248 Sizing up a log; 249-250 Sawing Wood to Width; 251 Planing Wood to Thickness; 252-253 Cutting Scarf Joint; 254-55 Scarf Joint Before and After Gluing

256

257

258

The frame blanks are now ready for steaming. Drum factories use industrial grade boilers (*fig 256*) hooked up to containers (*fig 257*) or steaming cabinets (*fig 258*) to prepare wood for bending. Steam cabinets generally contain shelves or racks that hold frame blanks away from pools of condensation and maximally expose the wood to steam. The length of time in the cabinet is variable depending mostly on the type and thickness of wood.

Another widely-used method of bending wood is by using a pinch roller. The pinch roller, sometimes called a mangle, consists of three rollers (fig 259), usually heated, configured so that when wet wood is drawn between them, one surface becomes compressed (slightly crushed) and the opposite surface slightly stretched resulting in curved wood. Often, the feeder roller has little teeth that engage the wood and force it through the apparatus leaving tell-tale indentations in the wood (fig 260).

259

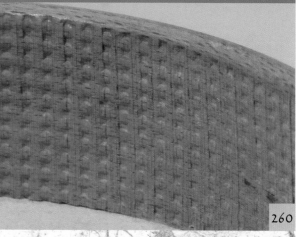

260

256-258 Steam Boiler and Steam Cabinets; 259 Pinch Roller; 260 Drum Frame Made With Mangle

261

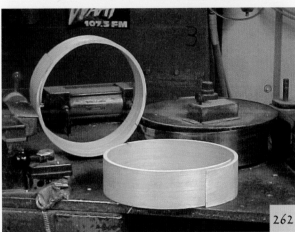

262

Once steamed, the frame blank is put into a windlass device that wraps or winds the blank around a circular block or mold of the desired diameter. Modern machines of this type are mechanically automated with heated blocks and metal back-straps that help wrest and fix the wood into its final shape *(figs 261-262)*. Large drum shells up to 9/16 inch thick can be bent this way *(fig 263)*. Older windlass machines *(fig 264)* from the Industrial era relied more on principles of weights and leverage to wrap wood around a block *(fig 265)*. Once bent into shape, the frame is temporarily secured and left until thoroughly dry *(fig 266)*.

264

265

266

263

261 Modern Wood Bending Windlass; 262 Bent Wood for Banjo Shells; 263 Bent Wood for Tenor Drum; 264 Industrial Period Windlass; 265 Feeding Wood Blank Into Windlass; 266 Drying Bent Drum Frames

The frame is then glued and clamped into its final circular configuration with a scarf joint. Thicker frames like those used in banjo shells (called pots) are built up from several layers glued together and clamped inside and out *(figs 267-268)*. Alternatively, drums with thin lightweight frames are often reinforced with support liners, strips of wood the same diameter as the frame glued around the inside circumference, thus adding more substance to the frame for extra strength.

Once the drum frame is intact, it is then sanded and finished *(fig 269)*. Most finishing materials work well. The bearing edge of the rim is slightly rounded and shaped to specification. A lip around the top portion of the frame is left unfinished so glue will adhere better when the skin is mounted.

267-268 Gluing and Clamping Laminated Banjo Shells; 269 Finishing Drum Frames

Drumhead Attachment

This project uses a simple basic method for skin attachment: gluing and stapling. After a medium to thick goat skin is cut to size and soaked in water *(fig 270)* glue is applied all around the edge of the rim where the skin will touch *(fig 271)*. The skin is then carefully centered on the frame and stapled into place using a crisscrossing pattern *(fig 272)*. Wrinkles and other irregularities are eliminated throughout this process.

How tight to pull the wet skin is a matter of opinion. Usually, since rawhide shrinks appreciably as it dries, some slack is left in the skin lest it get over-tightened. However, if the head is mounted too loose, it will be useless on humid or rainy days. Most makers let the head sag or deflect between 1/4 inch to 1/2 inch from flat.

Once staples are in place, a band is wrapped around the frame to cover the staples, help secure the skin, and give the drum a finished look *(fig 273)*. Excess skin is trimmed *(fig 274)*. Drying the head is done slowly to give the instrument time to adjust to new stresses and tensions.

270 Preparing Skin for Mounting; 271 Gluing Rim of Frame for Skin; 272 Stapling Skin to Frame; 273 Securing Skin to Frame With Cord; 274 Trimming Excess Skin

275

276

277

278

279

Sometimes wider fabric or wood banding is used to cover up staples and any ragged edges left from trimming the skin *(fig 275)*. Traditionally, tacks with decorative heads were attached all around to help stabilize the skin and add visual garnish.

Bodhrans invariably have either a single or double cross-handle installed inside the drum frame for holding *(fig 276)*. This can be as simple as a wooden dowel, or something more elaborate that has been turned on a lathe *(fig 277)*. Occasionally, the drumhead is decorated *(fig 278)*.

Beaters (called tippers) for playing the bodhran *(fig 279)* come in a variety of lengths and styles as seen in the accompanying figure *(fig 280)*.

280

275 Finished Bodhrans; 276 Bodhran Double Handle; 277 Lathed Single Handles; 278 Decorated Drumhead; 279 Player; 280 Bodhran Tippers

3 Middle East Drum

Although most Middle Eastern drums like the Egyptian tar, Uzbeki daf, Azerbaijani gaval, Turkish bendir, and Arabic riq are all characterized by a shallow circular frame with a relatively thin, glued-on goatskin *(fig 281)*, each has its own peculiarities. They are found in varying diameters, with and without jingles, each with its own special performance practice. Lightweight frames seem the rule not only for sound quality but because these drums are often held aloft in one hand while being played with the fingers of both hands. Drum frames are usually fashioned using steam bending methods or by bending with a pinch roller or mangle. For this project, I use yet a different construction approach for the sake of variety—gluing thin wood veneers together in plywood fashion *(fig 282)*. A cylindrical mold and band clamps are necessary in building up the frame thickness one layer at a time.

Drum Mold

Two circular mold and jig arrangements that help in gluing and clamping layers of veneers together are an adjustable-inside/fixed-outside style of mold and an adjustable-outside/fixed-inside design. In Irving Sloane's excellent book, *Making Musical Instruments*, a plan for building the former type is described in some detail. For my purposes, the inside mold is fixed and outside pressure is applied with a large metal band clamp *(fig 283)* and other auxiliary clamps as needed. Layers of veneers are built up until the specified rim thickness is reached.

281 Middle Eastern Frame Drums; 282 Laminated Frame; 283 Drum Mold and Band Clamp

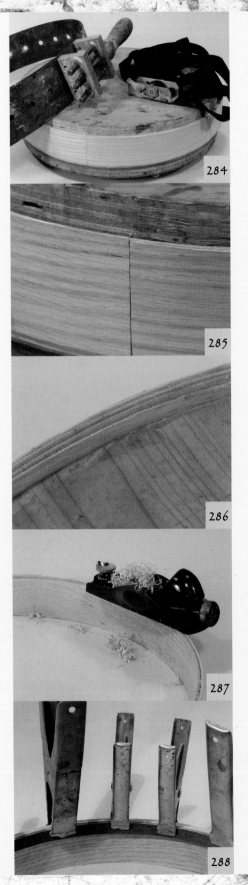

Drum Frame

Once the diameter and drum depth are determined, several lengths of wood veneer are cut and trimmed accordingly. Some species of wood veneers lie naturally flatter than others; the flatter the veneer, the easier it is to glue and clamp without it developing lumps and bulges. This drum frame is lightweight and designed to accommodate a thin skin: the frame is 2 inches deep, 16 inches diameter, and uses 8 layers of oak veneer built up to $\frac{1}{4}$ inch thickness.

The first layer of veneer (which will comprise the inside surface of the drum frame) is wrapped around the mold and temporarily taped end to end to hold it in place until subsequent layers are glued and clamped on top of it (fig 284). I prefer a slow drying epoxy glue which allows more work time, dries rock hard, and helps fill any small gaps that may occur between layers. Water-based wood glues work well but may make some veneers wrinkle or bubble. Small repairs are taken care of along the way. The ends of the final layer of veneer are trimmed carefully to make a neat connection (fig 285).

Once the frame is built up to the desired degree (fig 286), excess wood is trimmed from both rims with a plane (fig 287). For thin frames, it is a good idea to glue a reinforcing liner around the interior, head-side of the frame to help support the tension of the drumhead (fig 288). If a rawhide head gets too tight for the frame to support it, the frame will tend to warp into a banana shape. The frame is then cleaned up, minor repairs rectified, and all edges slightly rounded.

Clear finishes such as varnish or polyurethane are most appropriate on figured woods. In other cases, painting the frame is an easy alternative. Since the skin adheres much better to raw wood, masking tape is applied around the rim where the skin will touch the wood before applying the finish (fig 289).

284 Gluing Layers of Veneer Around Mold; 285 Trimmed and Glued Ends; 286 Removing Frame From Mold; 287 Planing Edges of Drum Frame; 288 Clamping Reinforcing Liner Inside Drum; 289 Removing Tape from Masked Rim Area After Painting

Drumhead Attachment

A thin goatskin will produce a sound characteristic to Middle Eastern frame drums: a clear tone with sharp response from strokes close to the rim. After the goatskin has been cut to size and soaked in cool water, glue is applied all round the frame and the skin secured, slightly slack, onto the drum frame with a band clamp. Wrinkles are worked out, excess skin trimmed with a razor, and the drum set aside to dry slowly *(fig 290)*.

Once dry, the drum is ready to play *(fig 291)*. A decorative band can be glued around the drum for added color and to cover any discrepancies.

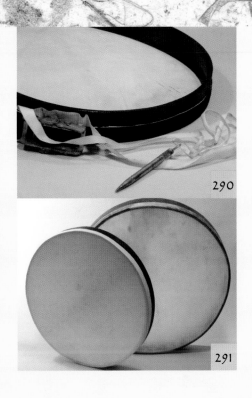

290 Gluing, Clamping, and Trimming Skin After Mounting; 291 Finished Drums

Many types of Latin American music and musical instruments—including guitars and accordions as well as drums—developed under combined input from European traditions and African influences. The basic form of the Latin American tambora most likely took its design from this Euro-African heritage. Tambora is actually a generic term used throughout Latin America to describe a two-headed, rope-tensioned cylindrical drum played with a stick, often in combination with a hand (fig 292). Regional differences are mostly in the dimensions of the drum shell, how the skin is attached (fig 293), and in its performance practice.

4 Latin Drum

Some drum frames are deep enough to be categorized as cylinders instead of frames. Deep drum frames are called shells. Historically prevalent in European music cultures, cylindrical drums are today commonplace as classical orchestral percussion, marching band instruments, and jazz and rock drumsets. Though folkloric, this tambora example makes use of contemporary resources and reflects how cylindrical drums are generally made today.

292 Tambora Player; 293 Tambora Project

Drum Shell

In some cases it is much more efficient for drum makers to use manufactured cylinders rather than build their own. Wooden tubes of all sizes and wall thicknesses are widely used in the architecture and construction industries for columns and pillars. One style of hollow cylinder is built from hardwood veneers laminated together under pressure. The cylinders are sturdy, can be cut to a specified length, and are mostly impervious to environmental conditions. Such structural fabrications also lend themselves to drum shell manufacture. Today, a majority of drum shells, from marching band drum corps to trap sets, are made using this resource *(fig 294)*. I will use a manufactured plywood cylinder that measures approximately 15 inches deep and 12 inches diameter.

Two flesh hoops and two counter hoops 1/2 inch larger than the diameter of the shell are prepared *(fig 295)*. The drum shell is sanded with special attention to rounding the skin-bearing edges around the rims of the cylinder. The shell is then finished by painting *(fig 296)* or with some other wood finishing. In the Latin spirit, the shell is sometimes quite colorful, painted with bright colors or wrapped in festive cloth.

Drumhead Attachment

See the Mali Weave description *(p40)* for more information on the following process. All the hoops are first spiral-wrapped with strips of cloth *(fig 297)*. An outline of the hoops is then transferred onto two goatskins leaving a margin of at least 4 inches extra all around for lapping the skin *(fig 298)*. Drumhead skins are cut to size in preparation for soaking *(fig 299)*.

Knots are tied at equal intervals around the two counter hoops in preparation for lacing using the Mali weave procedure *(figs 300-301)*. The last knot is finished off with a double weave as shown in the following figure *(fig 302)*.

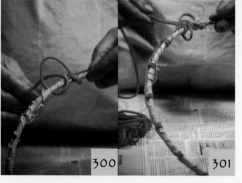

294 Laminated Drum Shells; 295 Preparing Drum Shell and Hoops; 296 Painting Drum Shell; 297 Wrapping Hoops with Cloth; 298 Marking Skin for Sizing; 299 Cutting Drumhead; 300-301 Tying Knots onto Counter Hoops; 302 Hoop Finishing Knot

The two heads need to be held firmly in place until laced. Since it is extremely difficult to keep two flesh hoops, two counter hoops, and two wet skins under control throughout this entire process, the soaked skins are temporarily mounted onto their respective flesh hoops until the lacing is in place. First, equally-spaced holes are poked all around the skin using a small nail *(fig 303)*. Then, with a needle and thread, the skins are sewn onto their respective flesh hoops *(fig 304)*. This step may seem extraneous but it is necessary to keep everything in place while the skins are moved onto the drum shell, the counter hoops placed on top *(fig 305)*, and the lacing begun.

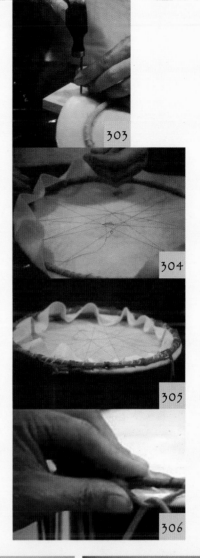

Once all hoops are positioned, temporary lacing between the two drumheads helps hold them in place throughout the lacing procedure *(also fig 305)*. Even then, constant attention must be given to keep the two heads centered on the shell until they are secure. Once set, excess skin is removed *(fig 306)*.

The drumheads are then brought to their final tension level by several rounds of rope tightening *(fig 307)*. When complete, a loop is tied in the end and the other end passed through it *(fig 308)*. A final knot secures the lacing *(fig 309)*.

A few weaves tidy up the loose end and excess rope is trimmed *(fig 310)*. In the case of nylon rope, the ends are burned to prevent unraveling *(fig 311)*. Add a shoulder strap, grab a stick, and the drum is ready for playing *(figs 312-313)*.

303-304 Securing Skin Onto Flesh Hoop; 305 Flesh Hoop and Counter Hoop Prepared for Lacing to Drum Shell; 306-307 Lacing and Tightening Drumheads; 308-309 Finishing Lacing Knots; 310-311 Trimming and Finishing Lacing; 312-313 Finished Tambora

5 Indian Drum

In recent years, the eight-sided, single-headed frame drum shown here has become a familiar style of Native American hoop drum (*fig 314*). The dimensions of hoop drums of this style normally measure 4 inches to 5 inches deep and 12 inches to 15 inches in diameter (*fig 315*). This project uses a construction method of mitering, a moderately easy woodworking technique that can be executed using fairly common tools.

Almost any wood or hide can be used although each material has characteristics that make it more or less well-suited for this type of drum. Cedar was used traditionally and continues to be the preference of many makers because of its light weight, straight grain, versatility, and availability. Other softwoods and hardwoods work equally well. And deer is the most commonly used skin, but elk, buffalo calf, cow, horse, caribou, sheep, goat, dog, and in more northern climes, walrus, and seal hides are not uncommon in Indian drum making. I used elk for this drumhead. It is substantial, supple, and resistant to tearing.

314

315

314-316 Native Drum Project

Drum Frame

A miter saw or power saw with an adjustable blade make cutting bevels easy. The blade is set to a 22 $\frac{1}{2}$ degree inclination, necessary for making an 8-sided frame. The length of each segment of wood determines the eventual diameter of the drum. This can vary depending on the size of animal hide and desired drum tone. After the first miter is cut, the wood is flipped over, measured to length and another miter cut on the opposite end. Each piece of wood will have converging bevels on both ends.

The eight pieces are then set up and adjusted where necessary for a good fit. Glue is applied to the end grain of each piece. A band clamp, large rubber bands, or other clamping strategy will hold the pieces in place while drying. I constructed this frame without splines or other reinforcement between the joints. The skin, when wrapped around the frame and dried, will provide the necessary forces to hold the frame together (fig 316).

316

Drumhead Attachment

To make the drumhead the animal hide is soaked in cool water overnight (fig 317). The drum frame is placed onto the center of the wet hide (fig 318) and measured to the desired size by adding the depth of the frame plus 2 inches around the outside of the frame. A spare piece of the frame (fig 319) helps with measuring. Excess hide is removed using scissors or a razor (fig 320). Scrap skin can be saved for making the lacing.

317
318

319

320

317 Soaking Elk Hide Skins; 318-320 Sizing and Cutting Drumhead

65

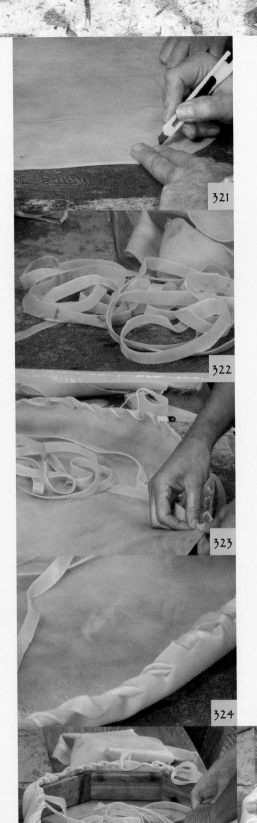

Short slits about two finger-widths apart are now cut all around the periphery of the drumhead approximately 1/2 inch in from the edge *(fig 321)*. The hide is then resoaked while lacing is cut from a scrap piece of hide. Lacing is best made by cutting a 1 inch wide strip in a continuous spiraling pattern *(fig 322)* and kept soaked until ready for using.

Lacing the drumhead is begun by threading lace through a slit, pulling the remaining length of lacing through that hole, spiraling the lacing around-and-through the next slit, taking up the slack *(fig 323)*, and proceeding in this fashion all around the head. As the lacing is pulled taut, the hide will begin to "dish" as shown *(fig 324)*.

Once the lacing around the drumhead is in place, the frame is placed onto the damp skin then overlapped and tightened bit by bit so that the head eventually begins to take the shape of the frame *(fig 325)*. The lacing is pulled tighter every pass around. Since a relatively heavy elkskin is used in this case, many passes are necessary until the head is stretched as tight as possible on the frame *(fig 326)*. A lighter deerskin or goatskin need not be pulled so tight at this stage.

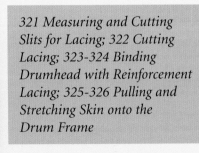

321 Measuring and Cutting Slits for Lacing; 322 Cutting Lacing; 323-324 Binding Drumhead with Reinforcement Lacing; 325-326 Pulling and Stretching Skin onto the Drum Frame

Drum Handle

Preparation for making the rawhide handle requires further stretching of the elkskin using strong string or cord (this step may be omitted if a thinner hide is used that more easily conforms to the frame). This process further tightens the head and keeps it centered on the drum frame for lacing. The string is strung back-and-forth across the drum *(figs 327-328)* in a 12 o'clock to 6 o'clock, 3 o'clock to 9 o'clock fashion.

Now the first rawhide lace is strung in similar doubled-up, back-and-forth fashion on top of the string, pulled tight and tied with a half-hitch knot *(fig 329)*. A separate length of hide lace is then wrapped around-and-around the first cross-lace in a spiraling configuration to build up and strengthen the handle *(fig 330)*.

The second handle lace is then strung at right angles to the first using the same procedure. It splits over-and-under the first lace as shown *(fig 331)*.

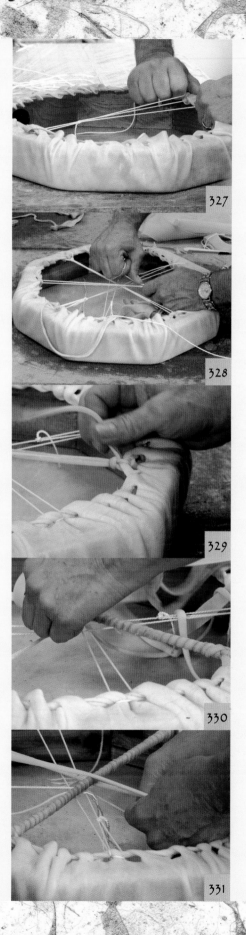

327

328

329

330

331

327-328 Further Stretching and Handle Preparation
329-331 Making the Drum Handle with Rawhide Lacing

332

333

334

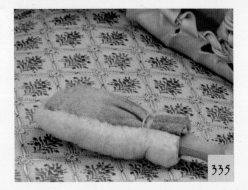

335

Once attached, it too is encased with another strip of lace. This process continues until all four cross-pieces of handle are in place *(figs 332-333)*.

An alternative method of making a handle is to make a central hub or disk of thick rawhide. An in-and-out "W" pattern of lacing makes for a sturdy and attractive handle as shown in the accompanying photograph *(fig 334)*. Wrapping the central grip with woolly sheepskin makes it even more comfortable to hold.

Once the handle is finished and everything is in place, the instrument is set aside in a cool environment to slowly dry. A beater or mallet for the drum is made from a 10 to 12 inch stick, some cotton padding, and tanned sheepskin or hide for a covering *(fig 335)*. The drum is then ready to play *(fig 336)*.

336

332 Making the Drum Handle with Rawhide Lacing;
333 Finished Drum Handle; 334 Alternative Drum Handle;
335 Drum Beater; 336 Making and Playing the Native Drum

⇜ Staved Drums ⇝

Some drum makers have devised methods to emulate the contours of barrels, cylinders, cones, and other shapes in ways that don't require the intense labor necessary to carve a drum from a solid log or steam bend staves into barrel shapes. This method of straight-stave construction is made possible by modern power tools, especially the table saw. Beveling slats of wood into staves and gluing them together edge to edge expedites the making of an interesting array of drum shell shapes.

For stave construction almost any kind of wood can be used—both softwoods and hardwoods are suitable. Considerations for wood choice include wood availability and expense (exotic woods cost more), durability (softwoods mar easier), workability (hardwoods can be more difficult to cut, craft, and sand), the eventual weight of the drum (hardwoods are heavier), and aesthetic considerations (wood color and grain configuration).

Three basic types of stave construction designs—cylindrical, conical, and compound conical shapes—can be made using the techniques described here. These drum designs are loosely based on those found in Mali, Senegal, Guinea, Gambia, and neighboring West African countries. Drums from these countries have become quite prevalent lately with cylindrical drums popularly called djun-djun (fig 337), conical drums called ashiko (fig 338), and compound conical drums called djembe (jem-bay) (fig 339). Given the polyrhythmic nature of African music, these drums are most often played in ensemble settings.

337 Cylindrical Drums; 338 Conical Drums; 339 Compound Conical Drums

Variations on a Bevel

Cylindrical drum shells are easiest to make because the staves are straight, not tapered. It is simply a matter of determining the correct degree of bevel on each stave relative to the number of staves used in the drum. More staves are usually necessary for larger drums; and the more staves, the rounder the drum shell will turn out. A general recommendation is that drums with a 9 inch diameter have 8 sides, 13 inch diameter drums have 12 sides, and drums 13 inches and larger have 16 sides. The final height of the drum is up to each maker. There are no rules with respect to how long a drum should be relative to its diameter. Generally, 3/4 inch thick stock is used since lumber is often milled to that measurement and it provides ample gluing surface.

For a 9 inch diameter drum shell with 8 sides, proceed as follows:

1 A circle has 360 degrees.
2 Each of the 8 staves is beveled on both sides resulting in a total of 16 bevels.
3 Divide 16 (bevels) into 360 degrees. The result, 22 1/2 degrees, is the angle necessary on both sides of each stave so they will fit together to form a cylinder.
4 To figure the width of each stave for making a drum with a 9 inch diameter, multiply 9 times pi (which is 3.14). The result is 28.26.
5 Now divide 28.26 by 8 (sides). The answer is 3.53. Rounded off and interpreted as inches, the outside width of each stave is thus 3 1/2 inches. This is all that is necessary to make a cylindrical-shaped drum.
6 With tapered drums, the lower opening is usually about one half the diameter of the head (a one to two ratio). For this drum, the small opening should be 4 1/2 inches in diameter. Multiply 4 1/2 by pi (3.14) with the result of 14.13. Dividing 14.13 by 8 (sides) equals close to 1 3/4 inches, which is the width of each stave at the base of the drum.

A commercial beveling jig or the jig design provided here can be used to cut tapered staves.

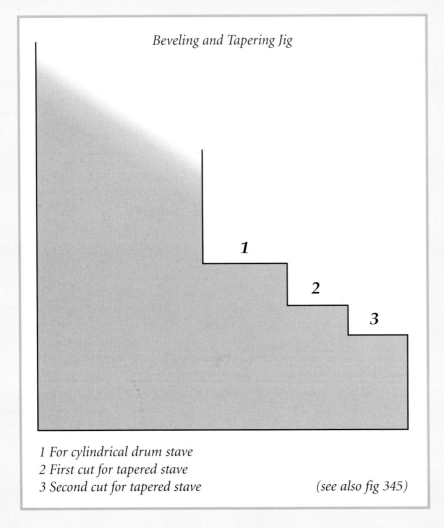

Beveling and Tapering Jig

1 For cylindrical drum stave
2 First cut for tapered stave
3 Second cut for tapered stave

(see also fig 345)

6 Cylindrical and Conical Drums

As seen in the above figures, drums of this sort come in various sizes. The following examples are based on the mid-size versions. The process begins by selecting several ³/₄ inch thick wood boards for processing *(fig 340)*. The length of the boards determines the eventual height of the drum which can be variable. In our case, they are measured and cross-cut to a length of 24 ¹/₂ inches *(figs 341-342)*.

Use a table saw or other power cutting tool designed to cut angles to bevel staves. In contrast to the conical drum, cutting staves for a cylindrical drum requires no special tapering jigs and less fine adjustment in fitting pieces together. For the cylindrical style, the saw guide fence is set to a 3 ¹/₂ inch width and the blade to a 22 ¹/₂ degree angle *(fig 343)*. Each board is pushed through, beveling one edge. Then, each stave is flipped over and beveled on the other edge so that the bevels, viewed on end, converge *(fig 344)*. Edges are then cleaned up and adjusted using a jointer or hand plane.

340 Stave Stock Rough Cut To Width; 341-342 Measuring and Cutting Stave Stock To Length; 343 Setting Table Saw Blade to Correct Width and Angle; 344 Staves for Cylindrical Drum Shell Cut and Ready To Glue

345

Cutting tapered staves for a conical-shaped drum requires a jig that will make the taper while maintaining a consistent bevel on both sides of each stave. The jig shown in the photograph *(fig 345)* is a simple and effective device for standardizing this process. Copy the design and measurements in the diagram above *(p70)* onto a piece of wood, cut it out, and follow this procedure to cut all the staves.

1 The width of the first notch determines the degree of a stave's taper. A larger first notch means more taper. The djembe, for instance, because it is built by connecting two different-size cones together, requires two different jigs.
2 For a conical-shaped drum, the second notch is for making the first cut to bevel and taper each stave *(fig 346)*.
3 Flip the jig end-over-end and utilize the third notch for beveling and tapering the second side of each stave *(fig 347)*. *(Notice in figure 345 how the third notch on the jig is itself beveled to accommodate the first bevel on the stave.)*

The angle of the saw blade may require modification up to ½ degree in order for all the parts to fit together seamlessly. Fine adjustments are worked out with a hand plane or on a jointer *(fig 348)*.

Gluing all the staves together requires some dexterity and is best accomplished with two people. Apply glue to one stave at a time or all at once, as shown *(fig 349)*.

346

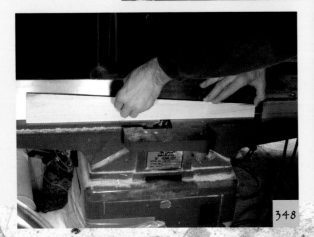
347

348

349

345 Jig For Cutting Tapered Staves; 346 Cutting First Side of Stave; 347 Cutting Second Side of Stave; 348 Truing Stave on Jointer; 349 Spreading Glue on Staves

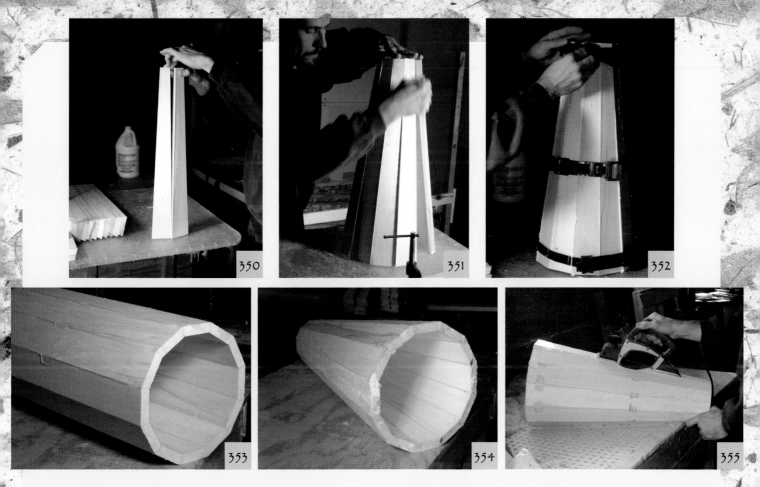

Staves are then assembled, band clamps applied, and adjustments made as demonstrated *(figs 350-352)*. After the glue has dried, the final shell for the cylindrical and conical drums should resemble the accompanying figures *(figs 353 & 354)*.

The shell is now planed, filed, and sanded with an electric sander or planer which expedite the removal of glue and transform the eight-sided vessel into a more seamless shape *(fig 355)*. The edge of the rim (bearing edge) is planed flat *(fig 356)* then rounded inside and out *(fig 357)*.

Once sanded, the wood is sealed and finishing coats applied. The degree to which the shell is finished is up to the builder. Drum makers sometimes lavish as much time on the finishing as on its basic construction. A fine finish adds to its ultimate quality. Most all finishes are effective if used as directed.

Refer to The Mali Weave *(p40)*, for details on mounting the skin onto the drum shell.

350-352 Assembling and Clamping Staves; 353 Completed Cylindrical Drum Shell; 354 Completed Conical Drum Shell; 355-356 Planing Sides and Top of Shell; 357 Rounding Skin Bearing Drum Rim; 358 Finished Conical (Ashiko) Drums

7 Compound Conical Drum

This project *(see fig 339)* is loosely based on the large, goblet-shaped West African djembe drum *(fig 359)* and uses the same basic construction techniques described for the conical-shaped ashiko drum described above. Traditionally, djembe drums are carved from solid pieces of heavy hardwood. Since drums with compound contours like the djembe demand more woodworking process than most, contemporary instrument makers have developed less laborious ways to replicate these drums. In fact, novel ways of making, decorating, and lacing these instruments are constantly being explored. Some modern djembes are even made using all synthetic materials and come in a wide variety of sizes.

Using stave-making techniques, drum shells can be made to closely resemble the basic shape of the traditional djembe. Although the general goblet shape is invariable, there is great variability of proportion, even among traditional djembes. In order to elicit the best tones from a drum, makers spend considerable amounts of time and energy on determining the optimum body size, shape, and proportion. Using a successful instrument as a model—and analyzing, adopting, and adapting its measurements—is a common practice among all instrument makers. Ongoing experimentation and constant adjustment are important and necessary elements in the process of instrument development.

In this case, the djembe is simply two different-sized, conical-shaped pieces, head and foot, joined at their small ends. The ratios and relationship between the two parts varies among drum makers. Primary considerations include 1) determining the relative sizes of the two components, 2) figuring the calculations for tapering the staves of the two cones so that they fit together seamlessly, then 3) securing the two components together.

359

359 Carved Djembe

The overall height of the most common size djembes is from 24 to 26 inches tall. The lower portion is sometimes a little longer than the upper portion but generally both parts are approximately the same height. Drumhead diameters range between 13 to 15 inches. The diameter at the waist is usually about ¼ the diameter of the top. The diameter of the base of the foot is slightly larger than the opening at the waist.

The drum shown here uses calculations based on a 16-sided drum with a 13 inch diameter drumhead. Using the basic jig design and procedures described in the making of the conical-shaped drum *(p71)*, all staves are cut, planed, and preassembled without glue so that adjustments to the top and bottom portions of the djembe can be made to fit nicely together.

However, getting the two components to fit together requires experimentation and tweaking. For instance, in the process of leveling the areas of contact between the head and foot to make a good flat connection between the two components, enough wood may be removed so that the two circumferences no longer match when put together. Some creative thinking and fine adjustment will improve most of these situations.

All the staves are then glued, clamped, and cleaned up as described with the conical drum example. Some makers then simply fit and glue the two components, foot and head, together. This works well as long as the top-heavy drum doesn't accidentally fall over and break the glue bond, a common mishap. Although more work, it is best to connect the top to the bottom more securely using dowels or screws to reinforce the glue. To do this, matching holes are drilled into both the top and base parts of the drum. First, equidistant holes are drilled into the end grain of the upper part *(fig 360)* so that they penetrate into the interior of the drum shell *(fig 361)*.

360

361

360-361 Holes Drilled into Shell of Djembe

Then the upper part is placed on the lower part and joined using glue and long screws to secure them together *(fig 362)*.

To use doweling instead of screws, the upper part has holes drilled as above and is then positioned onto the drum's base for guiding the drill bit into the base of the drum. Dowels are then inserted and glued into each connecting hole *(fig 363)*. Finishing material is applied at this stage.

Before the head and foot of the drum are actually glued together, the lower anchoring ring for attaching the string lacing must first be in place *(fig 364)*. Then it is time to begin attaching the drumhead using the Mali weave *(p40)*.

362 Screwing Top and Bottom Parts Together; 363 Dowels For Securing Top To Bottom; 364 Attaching Anchoring Ring For Lacing

❊Carved Drums❊

Cultural Perspective

Carving drums from solid wood is likely the most ancient and universal method of drum construction. Indigenous peoples in the Americas, Africa, Indonesia, Asia, Polynesia, and other culture worlds have all made use of nature's bounty in utilizing trees for their sound-making devices *(fig 365)*. And, since most all of these ancient cultures were of animist orientations, their instruments and the materials of which the instruments were made were usually endowed with spiritual attribute. They believed that the spirit of the wood and of the animal hide remained even after being changed from their natural form.

For many animistic cultures, tree cutting for drums is very serious business. Questions arise for those who are in charge of making drums. Are there cultural or spiritual strictures about which trees to use and which are prohibited? Are there particular individuals who are charged with the ritual of drum carving or can anyone carve a drum? Under what circumstances (time of year, special sacred space for drum carving , rituals and spirit appeasement, etc.) should trees be felled and drums carved? The same issues emerge regarding the acquisition of an animal skin. Every civilization, culture, tribe, community, or village may very well have different answers to these questions.

365

365 Carved African Drums

366

367

Ethnomusicologist Mantle Hood, in his classic documentary work in filming the making of a set of royal atumpan talking drums of the Ashanti people of West Africa, puts forth a fascinating account of how mandated the carving process can become. The making of the atumpan drums (fig 366) begins with careful selection of an ofema tree, a species of cedar (much harder than North American varieties) that grows deep in the rain forest and is highly esteemed by the Ashanti. Before cutting, libations are poured and ritual words spoken to appease the spirit of the tree. After felling, the tree is left to season for an extended period. The carving process is arduous and labor intensive and must be done only by a master drum carver (fig 367). Invocations to the wood and to the skin are unremitting throughout. The final decorative carving has great symbolic import as well with a symbolic eye carved on each drum facing important personages. When the drums are finally ready to play, Hood notes that "To watch the eyes of a master drummer as he tunes the atumpan, as he proudly demonstrates its technical requirements in playing, points out the symbolism in its shape or carving, tells you about its magic power, its connection with the ancestors, with the spirit of the tree that lives on in the drums, pours libations before each performance thereby honoring these spirits—to watch his eyes is a privileged reward of field work that no form of documentation can capture." Given a margin of variability, this scenario is not unusual in the world of traditional drum making.

366-367 Atumpan Drum Shell

368

369

370

371

372

373

374

375

I suspect that many of the first drums utilized the natural form and structure of the material used. Bamboo, coconuts, gourds, and calabash *(fig 368)* also fall into this category, the acoustic advantage being that they all have natural resonating cavities. Most all species of woods, however, are candidates for being fashioned into drums. Their selection for instrument making doubtless depends mostly on availability. The height and diameter of a tree may also dictate the size of the drum to some extent *(figs 369-370)*. The accompanying gallery of photographs provides some idea of how versatile a material wood is *(figs 371-375)*. Drum carvers will tell you that it is not the carver but the wood that guides the tool. Making a drum or any wooden instrument is a happy agreement between carver and the wood.

368 Calabash Drum; 369-375 Contrasting Drum Shapes

376

8 Drum Carving

Harvesting wood from the forest takes an extra degree of effort. There are actually few places left where one can simply go and cut down a tree. However, if one can find a tree that has died and been left standing for a year or two, it will save time in the seasoning and drying of the wood. If a tree is felled green and carved immediately, the chances of it checking, cracking, or even splitting wide open are greatly increased. One might be lucky enough to find a tree where insects have already accomplished most of the hollowing out leaving only a little cleanup to get things in shape. I often see trees in suburban neighborhoods that have been cut down, chain-sawed into sections, and ready to haul away. Sometimes these are very old trees that may be partially rotted in the middle thus prime candidates for a drum. The portion of

tree between its base and first limbs is best. An excessive number of knots or extreme irregularities in the wood grain lessen its potential since carving through knots is very hard work.

Once a section of tree is acquired, the wood must be seasoned, the slower the better. A section of green tree takes a long time to fully season before ready for woodworking. Softwoods dry quicker than hardwoods. The oft-quoted rule of thumb is one year of drying time per inch of wood. Some makers leave the bark on while others remove the bark so as not to invite infestation of bugs. Also, it depends on how the drum will look; some Native American drums leave the bark in place (*fig 376*). Leaving the bark on also retards the drying process which is generally a good idea.

376 Native American Water Drum With Bark

If the wood is dried out of doors, it should be kept in the shade. If it seems to be losing its moisture content too quickly, it can be wrapped in burlap and given an occasional sprinkle of water. If dried indoors, the section of wood is sometimes placed in a plastic bag and stored in a cool environment (like a basement). Opening the bag once in a while refreshes the air and discourages molding. Shellac, wax, or special sealants applied to the end grain of the wood is also a good way to slow the drying process and avert checking.

One traditional way of hollowing a section of tree is by controled burning with fire. Other standard methods usually involved hammering away with large chisels and gouges, a chunk at a time. Chainsaws and other power tools for chopping, hewing, and carving materials provide a more contemporary approach to log hollowing.

For two-headed drums, the wood section is naturally carved all the way through *(fig 377)*. Single-headed drums may require more accomodation because of how the drumhead will be attached and how the drum is meant to be held (under the arm, on a stand, with a shoulder strap, etc.).

The degree of finishing work is dependent on the desired outcome. Aside from rounding over the rim(s) that will receive the drumhead, the amount of filing, carving, and sanding depends on the type of drum and the intentions of its maker. As is known, decorative carving of the drum body is often an important part of the routine and adds an artful and often symbolically significant aspect to the drum *(figs 378-379)*.

Once the drum shell has been formed, it is best to seal the wood inside and out to help prevent possible weaknesses in the grain from suddenly fracturing. Shellac, wood finishing oils, or any commercial wood sealer should suffice. Finally, the drumhead is mounted as outlined in the Attaching Drumheads chapter *(p27)*.

377 Carved-Through, Two-Headed Drum;
378-379 Decorated Carved Drums

81

Clay Drums

The genesis of earthenware drums dates back into prehistory. Anthropologists agree that there is most likely a significant connection between clay crocks and jars used for storing grain and carrying water to drum manufacture. Shapes such as bulbous spherical containers are much easier to fashion from clay than to carve from wood *(figs 380-383)*.

380

381

382

383

380-383 *Various Clay Drum Shapes*

Goblet-shaped and jar-shaped hand drums are perhaps most pronounced in Middle Eastern cultures particularly across the Arabic world. North Africa, Egypt, Morocco, Turkey, Iraq, Iran, Armenia, Saudi Arabia, and Israel all have variant forms of goblet drums with regional names including darabukka, zarb, dorbak, derbekki, and tombak, but are most commonly referred to as dumbek (most notably in Egypt). These related drum types may be fashioned from various materials: terra cotta *(fig 384)*, wood *(fig 385)*, and metal *(fig 386)* and are often elaborately decorated with inlay or fancy metalwork.

For this project I use a shape generically based on Middle Eastern styles *(fig 387)*. Though traditional drums made of clay generally have glued-on heads with or without lacing and dumbeks with metal shells most always feature hardware tensioning devices, this project uses both lace and glue to secure the head to the vessel.

As always, the drum's size and shape have a lot to do with the resulting sound. This drum is approximately 12 inches tall with a head diameter of 8 inches and a foot diameter of about 4 1/2 inches. This ratio of head to foot is fairly common among goblet-shaped drums.

This project requires basic equipment used by potters: a potter's wheel for throwing the pot and a kiln for firing the clay. Other pottery tools used in fashioning the drum body include a needle tool for scoring and inscribing the moist clay, a wood knife for more intense incising, a wooden blade called a rib for overall shaping, controlling, and smoothing the clay, a trimming tool for more precise shaping, a small wet sponge for further smoothing, and a wire tool for detaching the clay from the wheel *(fig 388)*.

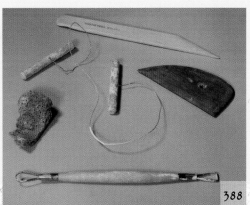

384 Clay Stoneware Goblet Drum; 385 Carved Wood Goblet Drum; 386 Metal Goblet Drum; 387 Clay Goblet Drums Project; 388 Pottery Tools

9 Goblet Drum

Throwing the Pot

The clay is first wedged and kneaded to work out bubbles and prepare it for the potter's wheel (*fig 389*). The drum body is built in two sections—the bowl-shaped top part which will receive the skin, and the cylindrical base or foot of the drum. Each section requires a five pound ball of clay. The base or foot is formed first.

The clay ball is carefully centered on the wheel (*fig 390*). It is then set in motion and patiently pulled up and shaped into a tapered cylinder, slightly flared at the bottom (*figs 391-392*). The opening at the top of the base is about 1/3 the size of the diameter of the actual drumhead. Once the cylinder is shaped, the rim is then flattened, compressed, and leveled so that it will join well when matched with the top part. The work is then removed from the wheel with the wire tool and set aside (*fig 393*).

389 *Wedging Clay;* 390-392 *Forming Clay for Drum Foot;* 393 *Removing Drum Foot From Wheel*

394

395

The upper bowl-shape portion of the drum is now formed using the same procedures *(figs 394-395)*. The bowl rim should be smoothed and slightly rounded *(fig 396)* then removed and set aside to dry.

The drum base is placed back on the wheel with its bottom positioned upward. It is carefully recentered with the needle tool *(fig 397)* and stabilized with wads of damp clay all around the lip *(fig 398)*.

397

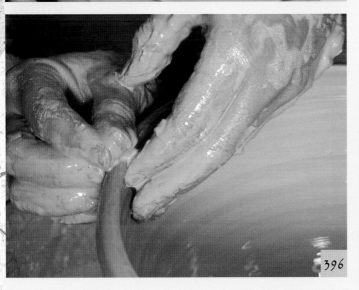

396

394-395 Forming Head of Drum; 396 Forming Bearing Edge of Drum Rim; 397 Recentering the Foot; 398 Securing the Foot

398

Excess clay in the center section of the foot is removed using the needle or knife tool *(fig 399)*. The inside, outside, and edge of the opening are then molded with the trimming tool so that the completed drum will sit flat and firmly when resting on its base *(figs 400-401)*.

This same procedure is followed with the bowl of the drum *(figs 402-404)*. The lower portion of the drum is now temporarily placed onto the the bowl as shown *(fig 405)* and the needle tool used to incise the outline circumference of the foot onto the bottom of the bowl *(fig 406)*.

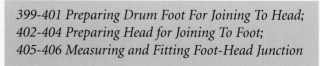

399-401 Preparing Drum Foot For Joining To Head;
402-404 Preparing Head for Joining To Foot;
405-406 Measuring and Fitting Foot-Head Junction

Excess clay is trimmed so that when they are joined, the transition from foot to bowl will be uniform, smooth, and seamless *(fig 407)*. With the needle and knife tools, the base of the bowl is then opened and trimmed to uniformity *(figs 408-409)*.

To insure a good bond between foot and bowl, the areas of connection on both foot and bowl are scored with the needle tool, as shown *(figs 410-411)*. A slurry of water and clay are dabbed along the parts to be joined *(fig 412)* and the two sections fitted together *(fig 413)*.

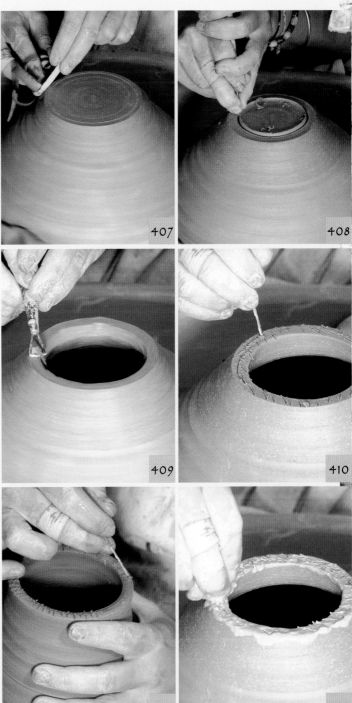

407

408

409

410

411

412

413

407-409 Sizing and Opening Head For Attaching Foot; 410-412 Preparing Components For Joining; 413 Joining Foot to Head

414

415

416

417

A thin coil of clay is prepared to help reinforce the connection *(fig 414)*. The joint is scored all around and a little slurry added *(fig 415)*. The clay coil is wrapped all around the joined area and smoothed to a final shape. The joint is reinforced on the inside of the drum using the same procedure *(fig 416)*. The drum is now ready for bisque firing, a first step before the glaze is applied *(fig 417)*.

The process of glazing is somewhat beyond the scope of this book. It is however, this element that makes the drum colorful, attractive, artful, and unique. There are many good books and other resources for information. Basically, a base glaze coat is applied *(fig 418)* over the whole drum shell then further enhanced by layering various colors and painting designs *(figs 419-420)*.

It is now ready for its final firing in a kiln *(fig 421)*. Wax is applied on the bottom and top rims of the drum to keep it from sticking to anything during the firing procedure.

418

421

419

420

414-416 *Securing Head To Foot;*
417 *Kiln for Bisque Firing Drum;*
418-420 *Applying Glaze and*
Decoration; 421 *Kiln Firing Drum*

Mounting the Drumhead

Tools for mounting the drumhead are shown here *(fig 422)*. The rim of the drum is sanded *(fig 423)* and a thin to medium rawhide goatskin prepared.

The rawhide head is cut about 5 inches larger than the circumference of the shell (18 inches in this case) to leave enough room for binding and lacing *(fig 424)*. The lacing for tensioning the skin anchors to a strip of rawhide tied around the vessel at the base of the bowl *(fig 425)*. For lacing, 15 to 20 feet of ¼ inch wide rawhide is cut and soaked in cool water for an hour until the hide becomes flaccid. In lieu of rawhide lacing, several kinds of manufactured lacing can be used. In this case, I have chosen a type of popular synthetic rawhide sinew used in leather working.

422

423

424

425

422 Tools For Mounting Drumhead; 423 Sanding and Smoothing Drum Rim; 424 Sizing Skin; 425 Attaching Anchoring Ring For Lacing

The skin is now postioned on the drum vessel and marks for the lacing holes are plotted about 1 inch apart and 1 inch outside the edge of the shell. Using a crayon or other nonpermanent marker won't leave an unsightly stain later. Concentric marks are now plotted 1 inch outside the first marks *(fig 426)*. Holes for lacing are poked at every marked point with an awl *(fig 427)*.

There are many different methods and patterns for lacing as described in Attaching Drumheads (p27). This should be thought through carefully as the style of lacing pattern determines the placement of holes. Here is a different lacing pattern, for example (fig 428).

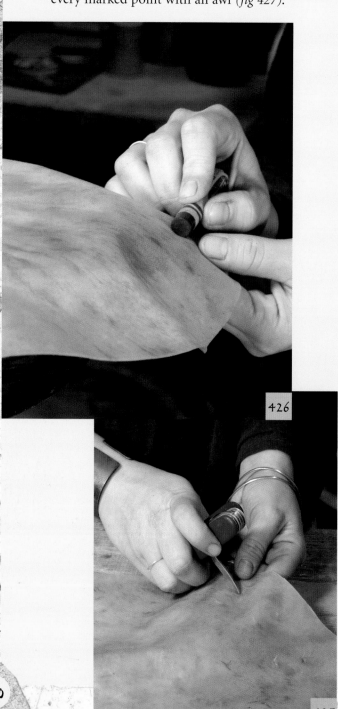

426

427

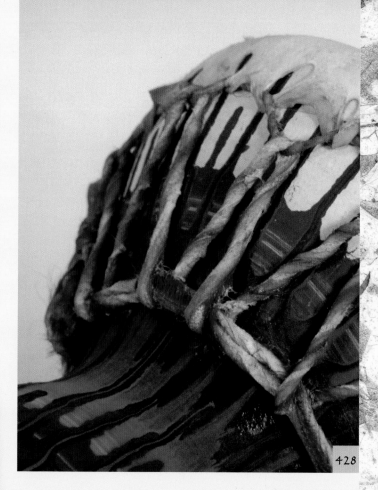

428

426-427 *Marking and Punching Lacing Holes; 428 Alternative Lacing Style*

A binding strip is cut which will encircle the drumhead, hold it in place, and support the lacing. White glue is spread around the rim of the drum shell *(fig 429)*, the skin centered on the body, and the strip of twisted binding, positioned between the punched holes, is tied snugly around the skin *(figs 430-431)*. The skin is pulled taut and wrinkles smoothed out in preparation for lacing.

429 Applying Glue to Drum Rim;
430-431 Fastening Drumhead To Body

432

Using a large embroidery needle, lace is passed up under the skin *(fig 432)*, through the top hole, over the binding, down through the lower hole *(fig 433)*, then down under the anchoring circlet at the base of the bowl, and back up-and-over to the next pair of holes in the drumhead, and so on *(fig 434)*.

Once laced, slack is pulled out a little at a time making sure the drumhead stays centered on the body. Excess skin is trimmed and the drum placed in an environment where the head can dry gradually. Once dry, it is ready to play *(fig 435)*.

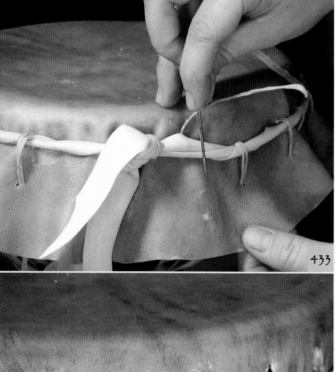

433

435

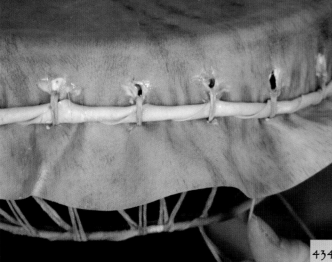

434

432-434 Lacing Drumhead To Body;
435 Finished Drum

About the Author

Dennis Waring is an ethnomusicologist, educator, performer, and instrument maker. He teaches education and world music courses, and performs in schools, universities, and other community-based institutions. His books Great Folk Instruments to Make and Play, Cool Cardboard Instruments to Make and Play, and Make Your Own Electric Guitar and Bass have delighted students and beginning instrument makers for many years.

Contributor Profiles

Matthew Broad and **Nathaniel Hall** (Staved Drums): Everyone's Drumming was founded in 1994. Co-owners Matthew Broad and Nathaniel Hall are dedicated to making and selling music related products that are of superior quality. They share their ideas and beliefs generously with the hope that they will create interest for others to make music and musical instruments. Through sharing , they believe that people will be more creative, better themselves, and ultimately help spread community spirit within our society.

Giovanni Ciarlo (Latin Drum): Giovanni Ciarlo is an artist, craftsperson, educator, and folklorist with extensive Latin American musical experience. He has lived and worked in Venezuela, Mexico, and the United States performing and teaching about global culture. Giovanni is a Connecticut Master Teaching Artist and a lead singer and arranger for the world music ensemble, Sirius Coyote. Giovanni and his wife Kathleen helped co-found an eco-village in central Mexico that is dedicated to developing energy alternatives and sustainable use of the natural environment.

James Dina (Primitive Drum): Jim Dina is a graduate of the U.S. Merchant Marine Academy and holds a MS degree from the Massachusetts Institute of Technology. He is a lover of nature and an accomplished outdoorsman with an abiding passion for primitive technologies. His interest was put to the test by building his own birch bark canoe with stone age tools, paddling the length of the Connecticut river, and writing a book, Voyage of the Ant, about his adventure. Jim also holds a degree from Hart College of Music and teaches classical guitar in schools and colleges.

The Cooperman Company (Irish Drum): The Cooperman Company is a second-generation family business founded by Patrick H. Cooperman in 1961 and presently managed by Patrick Cooperman, and Jim and Patsy Ellis. They blend the traditions of solid, bent-wood drum shell construction with innovations inspired by leading performing artists representing a variety of American, European, and Middle Eastern drumming traditions to create their finely crafted hand drums.

Shari Zabriskie (Clay Drum): Shari G. M. Zabriskie is a potter and drum maker as well as a gardener/ herbalist. Music and the arts is a central part of her family and community life. She states that "when making drums I am always mindful of the elements and energies which come together in the name of music as well as the healing and mirthful universality of the arts."

Paul and Maureen Gemme (Indian Drum): Gemme Innovations, owned and operated since 1990 by Paul and Maureen Gemme, is committed to providing some of the finest handmade drums and flutes found anywhere. Their instruments are built with passion and integrity and with the knowledge that each instrument has a spirit that speaks to its owner. In addition to drums and flutes, they also offer a variety of workshops for schools, corporations, and community groups.

Index